CONCILIUM
Religion in the Seventies

CONCILIUM

Religion in the Seventies

Volume 79: Spirituality

THE PRAYER LIFE

Edited by
Christian Duquoc and
Claude Geffré

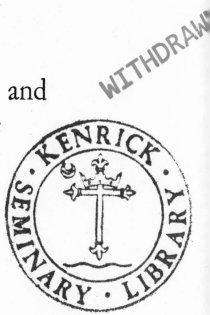

Herder and Herder

1972
HERDER AND HERDER NEW YORK
1221 Avenue of the Americas,
New York 10020

ISBN: 07-073609-x

Cum approbatione Ecclesiastica

Library of Congress Catalog Card Number: 72-3944

Printed in the United States

CONTENTS

PART III
DOCUMENTATION CONCILIUM

Editorial

PRAYER is no longer a common activity. Prayer is no longer one of the social attitudes recognized and accepted by the great majority. Prayer is now an original act, and makes a difference. Even believers find difficulty in justifying the practice; they don't like being different. Their forms of worship are evolving under the pressure of public opinion.

In the recent past Catholic worship included popular demonstrations. Believers asked God to prevent bad weather and to bless the harvest. These forms of prayer are fast disappearing. Some suspect them of sullying the purity of the faith, as being a gesture to magic. Others claim that they have no effect on men of our time, so incomprehensible are they to our mentality. No one any longer thinks of God intervening to transform the course of events.

It could be objected that this decline of the prayer of petition is not general. The official liturgy provides for a responsorial prayer in the celebration of the Eucharist called the universal prayer. It is a prayer of petition. The community places before God its wishes or worries, and lists the needs and sufferings of our age. The Vietnam war, underdevelopment, the threat of unemployment and the loneliness of the old are mentioned alongside spiritual requests. The growing collection of our sufferings, of injustices, crimes and catastrophes, forms the structure of official prayers. The prayer of petition is therefore very widespread. The form given it, even its very existence, nevertheless irritates many Christians. This prayer seems to them hypocritical if it is not associated with a political or trade union struggle to achieve the requests expressed. Others regard it as childish because it encourages an idea of God as the one who makes good the defects in our social systems. There is a crisis, reflected in blunt questions such as "What is the point of prayer?" Curiously, though, the crisis does not lead to indifference towards prayer, but makes people more interested in it.

The crisis, it seems, is the result of scientific and technical power over nature. Science and technology stimulate a different understanding of prayer. God is no longer the one to whom we turn to obtain extra power or protection against natural hazards. God is not a substitute for our social and political apathy; he does not make up for our neglect. The believer hardly dares to demand to be heard in requests for material goods. Prayer, even if it includes a specific request, is more than that request. It is the recognition that we are not spontaneously the inhabitants of the Kingdom promised by Jesus. It is the admission that we are not yet true children of God. The prayer of petition does not necessarily mean that the believer thinks of God as the donor who wipes off embarrassing debts or the power which makes up for our weakness. It is an expression, often clumsy, even more often naïve, on the occasion of real difficulties caused by separation from a loved one, illness, economic difficulties, the uncertainty of harvests, the danger of the roads, constantly recurring wars, sadness, loneliness, the death of friends, of the fact that we do not yet live in the Kingdom in which the protection and the love of God are manifest. They are promised in Jesus, but they are hidden. The prayer of petition is the cry wrung from believers by the delay in the fulfilment of the promise and the length of the wait. The cry which accompanies every petition is a response to the realization that evil is always at work and that the last enemy to be overcome, death, still has all his strength.

The Old Testament prophets cried out their impatience to see the promise fulfilled. The Old Testament believers expressed their hopes and weariness, their revolt or resignation. Jesus called to God in his trial, "Father, if thou art willing, remove this cup from me" (Lk. 22. 42). He did not ask for a miracle, he did not impatiently bring forward the coming of the Kingdom. He desired its coming with a great desire, and the New Testament reports that the primitive community made his desire its own: "Amen. Come, Lord Jesus!" (Rev. 22. 20). We do not yet live in the Kingdom, and the prayer of petition is the cry sent up to heaven, the cry wrung from us in the sight of God by our conflicts, our contradictions, our weaknesses and our sufferings, asking that the promise may at last be fulfilled. The cry will not go unanswered. John assures us: "I heard a great voice from the throne saying, 'Behold, the dwelling of God is with men. He will dwell with them, and they shall be his people, and God himself will be with them; he will wipe away every tear from their eyes, and death shall be no more, neither shall there be mourning nor crying nor pain any more, for the former things have passed away' " (Rev. 21. 3–4).

We do not live in the Kingdom, and our petition testifies to this. But we have to become children of God now. The prayer of petition attests not only that we are still far from the Kingdom, but also that we are not yet fully sons. Let us listen again to Jesus' prayer in Gethsemane, "Father, if thou art willing, remove this cup from me; nevertheless not my will, but thine, be done" (Lk. 22. 42). Jesus cries out to his Father. He knows what it costs us not to live in the Kingdom, but his cry to the Father is the request of a son. He prays like a son: not my will, but yours.

It is difficult to capture the true meaning of this prayer. Doing the will of God is such a disreputable expression, so clearly used as an instrument of repression, that it cannot fail to be irritating. It is especially ambiguous in the language of popular piety. It is easy to imagine a decree of God's to which we must submit, a legal prohibition, a pre-established plan, a worked-out blueprint. Matters are made worse by our ignorance of where the law can be read, where the plan can be consulted, the blueprint studied. Methods have been suggested: most recently, the signs of the times, previously, more naïvely, the authority of the Church. Vows of obedience in a religious congregation were a guarantee of a simple interpretative schema for the divine will. All these approaches to the meaning of the expression are unfortunate in varying degree; they give it a function which obscures its original meaning. God wants our freedom, and this desire is inseparable from his desire to make us his sons.

In Gethsemane Jesus asked God to remove the pain which was

looming over him, but added, "not my will, but thine, be done". The Kingdom has not yet come, and it is fitting for Jesus to cry out to God. It is no less fitting that the Kingdom should not come as a result of force; it is man set free. What God wants is this freedom coming from man himself, and not his negation or an imposed happiness, if indeed the two concepts, freedom and force, are compatible. It is not the satisfaction of desires which is the content of the Kingdom but the way in which man relates to that satisfaction. The satisfaction can only be the fruit of a freedom which has abandoned imaginary desires. Thus prayer becomes more urgent: signs of the times, laws, authorities, revolts, all show that we are not yet free and not yet children of God. The believer calls on God in order that Jesus' freedom as son may become his freedom; the believer begs God to give him the Spirit of Jesus so that he may be converted. Prayer is the act by which one abandons oneself in order to let oneself be seized by the freedom of the Spirit. The cry forced from us by our suffering because the Kingdom has not come, or by our alienation because freedom is a promise, expresses our situation before God; we do not require of him either an increase of power or a privileged status, but the freedom which comes from the Spirit. Paradoxically, we ask him for the power to be ourselves by allowing him to be God for us. In this way we become sons, that is, capable of not being in any way rivals of the Father, responsible for ourselves, open to love.

These very brief remarks show that prayer is inseparable from the act of conversion. It starts in a request which tends to make God the omnipotent repairer of our practical and technical inadequacies. At that stage it is egocentric and a prisoner of our worship of utility. It does not listen, it chatters; it tells God all about us. But gradually prayer changes its tone. It stops being obsessed with our wants and our needs; it becomes silent, enters the night, and God seems to fall silent. The believer then really understands that God is not the necessary supplement to his actions, any more than the human father is the power which makes up for the weakness of his son. God is the one who urges us to risk our freedom in a unique adventure, and in the process he is the one who shows us his face in Jesus. The present silence of God is not a void; it is the condition for the proclamation of a word always present but none the less forgotten, the evangelical word of which Jesus was the prophet. The present silence is a preparation for the hearing of that word; it is creating a taste for it. The silence of the present is the possibility of recollection in order to understand what was said and what the Spirit is whispering in us. In this way man grows in the act of prayer. He acquires a new relation to beings and things. He is no longer obsessed with production, but opens himself to the outpouring of a richness which comes from outside himself and which his appetite for power and manufacture had made him forget.

The new attention given to prayer also influences the way in which men see their relation to the world. Our industrial civilization is often accused of being predatory. It exploits nature and men to satisfy superficial or artificial needs. The process destroys not only the environment but also the quality of life. There is a growing suspicion of science, in the eyes of many the major factor in this irrational growth and organized depredation.

It would be naïve to use these revolts or these signs of impatience as the basis for an apologetic, and it would be equally naïve to offload onto science the responsibility for the unfortunate consequences of our social organization or our lust for material wealth. The imperialism of the scientific outlook fills a vacuum. If Western man is no more than a producer, it is undoubtedly because his culture and his thirst for power point him in that direction. Prayer itself was for a long time a technique for domestication. At the moment when our technical mastery reaches its peak the disappearance of one of the functions of prayer allows us to see its full dimensions.

Praying to God thus has practical consequences. They exist in the measure that they are not sought; they belong to the surplus which stems from free giving. This issue of *Concilium*, in spite of the wide range of opinions presented, will have fulfilled its purpose if it makes the constant question, "What's the point of prayer?", superfluous and if it points towards a relation to the world which is the result or a foretaste of the freedom of the Spirit.

CHRISTIAN DUQUOC

PART I
ARTICLES

Jean-Claude Sagne

Coming to Terms with the Father: Prayer and Psychoanalysis

BY THE very fact that it is the act of faith searching for God, prayer has a human meaning, a meaning which is closely allied to the relation of intersubjectivity in speech. It has, however, two characteristics which distinguish it from normal conversation between men. First, prayer reveals to the believer the paternity of God and establishes an original link, in that man recognizes his dependence on one who is the pure gift of self and absolute origin of everything. Between man and God there is neither similarity of situation nor total reciprocity. In addition, the conversation which is prayer can apparently take place in the silence of the night or the solitude of the desert. The one to whom the words are spoken remains in himself invisible and silent. These two features explain each other; it is precisely because God is Father that he reveals himself in silence and darkness.

Into this uniqueness, prayer inserts a specific human meaning. It teaches us that man discovers his personal identity in the measure that he recognizes the otherness of the other, which takes place primarily in the relation with the father when a person accepts himself as that father's son. This relation of reciprocal revelation has a movement of its own, which takes us from knowledge of ourselves to acceptance of ourselves and recognition of the other. We shall try to reflect on this process by comparing it with psychoanalysis, in which the patient sets off in search of the true image of his father and of his identity as a son and in which his only equipment is words addressed to a silent analyst whom he cannot see.

I. SELF-KNOWLEDGE

The segmentation of social life gives added urgency to the need to reunify personal life by turning in on oneself, collecting together one's whole being, thus putting a temporary end to dispersion in the multiplicity of relations and tasks.

This reunification of the self cannot take place in action or in purely intellectual discussion. A characteristic of any action directed at the performance of an external task is that it includes a defensive aspect; by acting we avoid a more immediate encounter with another person, we protect ourselves against our desire by going forward to meet it. This means that we cannot re-create the unity of our personality by our work, any more than we can by investigating ourselves theoretically and in the abstract through mere rational confrontation with books or ideas. This intellectual self-knowledge cannot overcome the diversity of our contradictory desires or elucidate our unconscious conflict.

Our reunification can only come from working on ourselves in the order of desire and love. The deepest source of our fragmentation is in our desire, and that is why work on our will is capable of reunifying us. Consciously locating and explaining our desires is not enough; we need to accept their existence affectively and let them rise to the full light of consciousness. In other words the task is to discover and establish a better psychic compromise. The synthesis of the personality is in this way connected with a practical knowledge, in the form of acceptance and affective presence to oneself.

This task of spiritual reconciliation can only be performed in the act of speech. Speech itself has a reconciling power. For the purpose we are discussing, of course, we need a word in which we express ourselves completely and put ourselves in the other's hands.

When it is genuine and complete, speech can reconcile. It is already in itself affectivity and intelligence, presence to the self and given meaning. It is not content, however, merely to use these various registers; it puts them together. It is not just simple expression, but presence to oneself through presence to others. It is speaking to the other that makes it possible for us to exist in a coherent and unified way. To bring this about, it is obviously necessary for the speech to be really addressed to another, whose presence is, at the very least, an implicit hypothesis or a hoped for possibility.

Without this real orientation towards the other, whether he is present or expected or imaginary, there can be no reconciling speech, but only a meditation on oneself which refines the conscious image of the self without at all modifying the latent conflict. Reunification of oneself requires recollection and freedom from desire, and this is impossible without a complete and trusting surrender of oneself to another; this takes place fully in the act of speaking to another, as in the promise of perfect faithfulness in marriage or in religious profession.

This seems the natural setting for human conversation in human love, but what about the words spoken in prayer, when the other remains silent and invisible and gives no tangible signs of reciprocity? This is what we shall try to work out from the example of the comparable case of psychoanalysis.

What makes free association possible for the patient is the silence and the analyst's withdrawal from his field of vision. The situation of psychoanalysis is completely unique, with possibilities open to no other social relation. As soon as the other person responds to me with movements or words, or as soon as I can see his reactions in his face, free association becomes impossible. I can no longer follow the train of my ideas and images without interrupting it or diverting it, but inevitably make a selection in what may come into my mind, guiding myself in function of the desire I ascribe to the other from what he lets me see of him. The very fact of seeing the other in a face-to-face conversation is an embarrassment, because I shall be afraid of saying everything for fear of his look, which will reinforce the self-accusation of my super-ego. In verging on absence through his neutrality, his withdrawal and his silence, the analyst encourages the most complete possible verbal expression. By refusing the satisfaction of love which I demand of him and by not reinforcing me through the assertion of my worth or supplying objective information, the analyst pushes me further and further and makes me reveal my desire more clearly. The absence of action, which would embody and conceal the desire, leads to its verbalization. Through this the desire gradually reveals its mental structure by gradually releasing the details of the imaginary and unconscious scenes which are the cage in which it threshes.

Speaking to this off-putting and unresponsive other person who is the analyst gives a self-knowledge which, while very slow and very partial, is none the less the only serious interpretation of our unconscious.

We could push the situation of analysis to its limit. Since the analyst encourages self-knowledge by his silence and his absence, which are none the less only relative, would not his disappearance give the patient total freedom? We are now in the realm of the absurd, and this throws light in retrospect on the procedures of therapy. Talking to oneself in an empty room would be a totally repetitive monologue, alienating and with no development. Without a real reference to another, speech encloses the subject within his own imagination. In that situation the image of the other is no more than the projection of desire and aggression, a faithful impression of the psychic structure of the subject who thinks he is talking to the other when he is in fact only talking, about himself, to himself.

It is not the absence of the other which frees expression and gives speech force, but his presence when it takes on the force of an appeal through his withdrawal and silence. Withdrawal before me which is at the same time clearly present has the effect of inciting my desire. This is not the hide-and-seek of seduction, but the refusal to give any foothold in order to free the other person's ability to walk alone and take full responsibility for his life. In this situation distance is offered as a space to be explored and conquered.

There is a proof *e contrario* that the analyst's presence is necessary and stimulating in the ambiguities and traps in the patient's words, produced by the patient's tendency to nullify the presence of that other whom he cannot see and does not want to hear, in order to reduce him to a pure absence. This means that the analyst points the patient back to the glaring evidence of his narcissism, as illustrated by his techniques for avoiding others. Every means is fair for the patient in his attempt to put up a screen between himself and the analyst, even the words he speaks to him, in an effort to disguise and confuse the other's words.

This evasion is prevented by the presence of the analyst, which cannot be suppressed; it is always to him that one talks, even if one can only talk about oneself. Even more than by his presence alone, the analyst recalls reality by the few words in which he does no more than say in his own way what the patient has said in order to enable him the better to hear and understand himself. He has no other power or desire than to listen to what the patient says with a trained mind and better clarified desire. In the interpretations thus produced the patient hears his own words spoken openly and clearly, by himself or the analyst, and discovers what he "means", his meaning. He comes to himself through the words of another, who gives him back his own words with a new understanding and freedom.

If we now pass from the situation of analysis to the conversation which takes place in prayer, we find, among the positive elements, free association of ideas and free expression of desire. This freedom would seem to be even better guaranteed in this case by the complete silence and complete absence of the other at the level of appearances. However, these are precisely the elements which make the situation in prayer the reverse of analysis. Talking to this person who is absent without hearing his reply, and indeed without expecting it, can be a narcissistic refuge to avoid the encounter with reality and others: one has created an imaginary partner who is merely one's own idealized double. To prevent his protests against the traps in our images and words, God becomes for us the product of our desire, the projection of our ideal of the ego, or the product of our aggression, the projection of our super-ego.

Paradoxically, it is the practice of prayer as talking to God which may constitute an obstacle to a meeting with the living and true God and the hearing of his word of power. Unknown to himself, the worshipper may construct a sort of spiritual atheism in which representations of God and types of prayer become too infiltrated by the imagination and become defences against the presence of God and obstacles to his free intervention. Even the language of prayer may deteriorate into noise and blur the word of God, which can only be heard in silence. Our belief that we are in intimate and privileged communication with a perfect being who assures us of his love and approval may conceal from us our inadequacy and our failings, and function as a narcissistic reassurance. We may be cutting ourselves off from the signs of our weakness and our failures which would open the door of our hearts to the action of the Holy Spirit. Self-knowledge in such a situation is full of illusions and conceals a very partial unification of the personality, based on contempt for or mutilation of pressures feared by the ego.

These spiritual ambiguities cannot be completely overcome by the practice of prayer alone, although it would do no good to use them as an excuse to stop praying until such time as authentic communication with God were restored, as if by magic. That would simply be a rationalization of a desire to give up prayer. Our criticisms are simply intended to show the need for and value of new spiritual inventiveness. The truth of an intersubjective relation is never there ready-made from the beginning, but always the term sought by an effort of authentication, like an ultimate goal not yet reached and for that reason a stimulus.

The relation of man to God in prayer is no exception to this need for constant work to produce and perfect the truth of the conversation. Such efforts are normally made in twos, and in addition with the help of an outside witness in the role of demystifier and reminder of reality. In this sort of task of authentication it is obvious that a breach with the other is a serious obstacle to the rediscovery of the truth, and not an encouragement, because the persistent conflict with the other through his absence fosters the productions of aggression and the imagination. If language is indeed the source of misunderstandings, the fox would have been very wise to warn the Little Prince equally against the ambiguities of silence, which are even more serious because there is no possible help within the silence. On the contrary, it is the patient pursuit of verbal conversation which makes us able to overcome, little by little, the seductive and disturbing delusions of the imagination through a liberating confrontation with reality.

In any case prayer does not dispense us from living and working in order to obtain the substance of a genuine offering from among our freely chosen actions and relationships, any more than psychoanalysis can do without the other relations of life, without which there would be nothing to analyse. In addition to the authentication which comes from the practice of brotherly love, however, prayer has a more specific means of regulation within itself. The more I talk to the divine Other, the more I realize that I am not really talking to him and that I do not know him. By becoming more sharply aware of my desire, my true condition, my spiritual experience as the basis of my vision of God by faith, I acquire a negative knowledge of God which reveals him to me in a reversed image. I get a stronger and stronger impression that he is different from my desire and that he cannot be exhausted or circumscribed by my ideas, images or attitudes. This constantly developing awareness, as I mature in prayer, of the distance which removes God beyond my representations and emotions forces me more and more to desire and search for the presence of God beyond words. I grow to love him as he is and for what he is, no longer with an anxious desire which devours its object, but with trusting and humble expectation of his free coming at the hour of his choosing.

God's failure to reply to my requests no longer seems indifference, but a sign of his freedom and gratuitousness. His failure to intervene betrays not weakness or complicity, but patience and teaching. His silence is not dumbness, but a discreet reminder of a unique and complete word, to which God has nothing to add for our personal use because it has been spoken completely once and for all. It is my task to open the book which contains this word and to receive the living witness of the Church which reveals the word's saving effect in history. It is my task to listen to this word in God's presence, to make it my own by interiorizing it and adding my own word to it in order to anchor it in the most existential reality of all.

Perseverance in the practice of prayer shows us more and more clearly the otherness of God, which bursts out especially in the crises and conflicts which confront our desire for happiness and a life seeking God. God now has no need to say another word to us apart from the mystery of Jesus in order to point us towards the reflection of our desire in events and meetings. The holiness of God, which is the perfection of his love and the irrevocable fullness of his unchanging mercy, acts as a mirror for us. God does not look on us from the outside, either to please or condemn us. It is enough for him to be what he is and to make known his love, to reveal to us what we desire and what we are.

The presence of God, interpreted through the message of revelation and the events of life, makes prayer the source of a knowledge of ourselves by bringing to light our desire. Psycho-analysis has given us a comparison, but the limits of this need to be suggested. The analyst is not the authorized witness of any ethical demand or any spiritual truth. He has no word to speak in his own name; he has accepted the task of listening to and repeating the words of the other, the patient, which is in any case the best way of getting the patient to purge his desire of the products of his imagination, but he does not predetermine the way in which the patient will then deal with his desire, satisfy or sublimate it. The word of God, on the other hand, has an original and positive content which reveals the most real reality and con-stitutes the deepest law of our development. Not only does it present our desire with a demand, but it also works at the heart of our desire, criticizing it from within and opening it from within to this demand. The psychotherapist is not an outsider to the extent that he does no more than point the patient back to his own desire, without making any sort of contribution from outside. The Holy Spirit does not sanctify us from outside our-selves for the very reason that he is the source of our identity. As such, he does no more than continue his creative action by edu-cating our hearts in prayer in order to show us more clearly our end and make us move more surely towards it.

II. Self-acceptance and Recognition of the Other

1. Self-acceptance

The self-knowledge obtained in prayer is not like a static in-ventory, but more like a stimulus to change. It goes with a spiritual reunification by which we agree to the existence of all that is in us. Self-knowledge leads to and makes possible self-acceptance. This does not mean approving of what we are or resigning ourselves to it; accepting oneself means a search for more clarity, having a sound judgment and being patient with oneself. It is this form of self-acceptance which proves to be the most important factor in changing the personality.

It is only if we are not afraid of ourselves and of our unconscious and do not deny the right of its impulses to exist, that we can integrate everything into our personality through a positive and unifying attitude. This makes us more able to identify ourselves with the other and above all with the parental figure and this in turn stabilizes our legitimate self-satisfaction. The subject is more secure and independent, better able to make decisions and to bear the dependence involved in affective relations with the other. The more completely we accept ourselves, the less we shall fear the presence of the other as a threat. This presupposes that we accept our inadequacy and finitude, our limitations and our death. This is affective freedom. By clinging to our real identity without illusions and therefore without pain, we become freer to accept the other.

Self-acceptance can only really take place through speaking and listening to the other. In psychoanalysis this acceptance means that I try to say everything, including my negative and aggressive feelings, to the psychiatrist. I accept myself to the extent that I am able to verbalize what was most painful to say and so most deeply embedded.

There is, it is true, a danger that by going too far in this direction one falls into a perverse exhibitionism or a depressive self-depreciation. Choosing to dwell on the degrading or immature aspects of the personality conceals, however, violent feelings of aggression towards the therapist, whether as an attempt to defy him or to abase oneself before him. These are some of the strategies we use to entice him and trap him in our game. Becoming aware of this ambiguity should lead self-acceptance towards truth and joy.

Prayer leads to self-acceptance by allowing us to express and explore our desires. This is proved by the peace often brought by prayer. However, the increased frequency of the demands of the ego-ideal or of the prohibitions of the super-ego through the guarantee demanded of God threaten to over-emphasize self-criticism. Scruples and doubts are rich in narcissism and aggression and leave little room for thinking about God's love for man. Meditation on divine mercy may in this context seem a good counterweight for the temptation to self-rejection. The unique possibility of prayer, from the point of view of analysis, is this positive affirmation of the love of God, which, by providing real security, makes self-acceptance easier.

2. *Recognition of the Other*

The correlative of self-acceptance is recognition of the other. Self-acceptance is both the cause and result of recognition of the other. There is a circular causality between the two. Recognition of the other means admitting him and even actively postulating him as other than oneself and different, as a subject of liberty and desire, who wants to exist in his own right and choose his future. It means wanting the other and making him exist in his fullest identity and his most personal difference, in that which most distinguishes him from others and from my own desire. Recognition of the other means making him the gift of oneself and revealing to him his original vocation. This involves telling him everything that one expects from him, but giving up all that one desires from him.

The result of recognizing the other is to make him completely free in relation to ourselves, to the extent that we give ourselves completely to him in a surrender of ourselves which tries to be complete and trusting, without making any demands. This gift of oneself to the other in dependence and love softens the urgent call of spontaneous desire and prepares the way for a humble, peaceful and disinterested welcome which tends to become pure presence to the presence of the other.

Once again it is through speech that this recognition of the other takes place, through speech which is stamped with the desire for reciprocity. Both the conversation in psychoanalysis and that in prayer seem, however, to deviate considerably from the most typical forms of mutual recognition, which is the human relation of love. If there is a reciprocity in analysis and prayer between the speaker and the one who is addressed, this reciprocity, however real, is not given explicit expression. The other does not respond to the demand for gratification by expressing desire as in a relation of love. He refuses to repeat specially that he feels admiration or affection, and does not provide the portrait or the estimate demanded.

Both these conversations, which are marked by a dissimilarity in the condition of the partners, produce a recognition of the other, but in a characteristic way related to the trace left by silence and absence. The other is apprehended as a reversed, negative image. This is precisely how the other reveals himself as other than desire in its immediate inclination. Confronted with a person whom it cannot grasp, desire is invited to leave the maternal approach which promises immediate satisfaction of the need for security and love in order to move on to a new way of operating based on the distance of the object and the need for social mediations to obtain it. It is the father's role to lead desire to this change of attitude, and he must be prepared to be seen at any moment as a brutally repressive and frustrating tyrant. However, it is by cutting the child off from its love-object, the mother and then her substitutes, that the father, by revealing to desire the otherness and difference of reality, works to free the child's desire by giving him the chance of structuring himself on identification with his father.

It is on the lines of this symbolic function undertaken by the father that we are to understand the form of absent presence which is that of the analyst or of God. By making the patient re-live the conflict with his father, the analyst gives him back the chance of being reconciled with his father and finding his identity by interiorizing his father's words. By offering no other revelation than that which he gave once and for all, God manifests the superabundance of his love in his discretion and the totalizing nature of his presence in his apparent absence. He is invisible because he is the source of all light, and silent because he is the origin of the complete word of Jesus. In receiving this word as the law of his development, man finds his identity by recognizing the Father and accepting himself as a son. In order to do this he has to make himself really present to the invisible and silent presence of the Father. This is the real efficacy of the conversation which is prayer, when the worshipper models his own words on the words of Jesus, which is not so much a request as an invocation and confession of the Name of the Father: "Abba, Father!"

Translated by Francis McDonagh

Michel de Goedt

The Intercession of the Spirit in Christian Prayer (Rom. 8. 26–27)

"THE Spirit helps us in our weakness in the same way; for we do not know what to ask for to conform to the requirements of true prayer, but the Spirit himself intercedes with wordless groans, and he who searches the hearts of men knows what is the aspiration of the Spirit, knows that he intercedes for the saints according to (the will of) God" (Rom. 8. 26–27).

Romans 8. 18–30 contains many difficulties, and not the least of these are the exegetical questions raised by 8. 26–7. In apparent contradiction to his invitations and encouragement to pray, Paul in these verses maintains that we are not capable of praying to God "properly",[1] and that the Spirit makes up, as it were, for our inability by interceding for us. Inability to pray "properly" and the intercession of the Spirit are ideas which are not expressed elsewhere in the Pauline epistles, nor in the rest of the New Testament. Such is the strangeness of these ideas that many writers try to soften it, if not to remove it completely—according to them, inability to pray is not radical, but partial and temporary, corresponding to what the manuals of spirituality used to call "difficulties in the life of prayer" or "dryness in the devotional life". In the gift of the Spirit so that we can pray

---

[1] "Properly" may be misleading. The text says nothing about knowing in what way to pray; the problem is the conformity of prayer of petition with the "requirements" of its object, which is the will of God or, more precisely, his "purpose" (Greek *prothesis,* 8. 28) as described in 8. 28–30. In the Greek, the phrase "according to (the mind of) God" (*kata Theon,* 8. 27) picks up and interprets the phrase in 8. 26 here translated "properly" (*katho dei*).

"properly" some writers see an instance of Christian *oratio infusa*, similar to the prayer of that name encountered by religious historians in their work.

What all these interpretations have in common is that none of them is based on the text itself. In my view the new desire to pray which can be seen among Christians today and which has sometimes been called "the return of the Spirit" requires us to examine this passage. It may be that the word of God to which this passage bears witness will give us valuable assistance in testing spirits in the present proliferation of experiences and aspirations. A text whose meaning puts us off, or which appears at first sight not to fit in with our present attitudes, may ultimately be more timely than other texts more immediately acceptable to our taste.

The Context

Rom. 7. 7–25 is the reply to the second objection provoked by the theology of the righteousness of God, the righteousness which has been revealed in the Gospel for the salvation of all men, Jews and Greeks. Paul has shown that, having died to sin, we cannot continue in sin so that grace may abound (6. 1–7), and this leads him into a formal discussion of the Law, which came into the reply to the first objection. What connection is there between sin and the Law? Paul replies that a sort of law of sin took advantage of the "Law of God" to reveal itself and kill those whom it misled. This reply, which applies to those who are not in Christ Jesus, requires the argument of Romans 8 as proof of the opposition; it requires that the overcoming of this opposition should be clearly shown—the law of the spirit of life has freed us from the condemnation attached to the law of sin and death.

The argument of the chapter is in three parts. The Spirit of him who raised Jesus from the dead lives in us, and our actions are performed, or ought to be, under the guidance of that Spirit, who aspires to life and peace (8. 1–11). We must put to death, by the Spirit, the deeds of the body if we wish to receive our inheritance as sons of God and fellow heirs with Christ (8. 12–17). The glory to which we are predestined is completely certain and bears no comparison with the sufferings of this present time, in the midst of which we groan as we wait for the redemption of our bodies (8. 18–30). These considerations on the life and hope of those who have the Spirit of Christ are followed by a peroration introduced by a series of urgent questions, all intended to lead into the multiple affirmation that nothing can qualify the certainty of this hope, and Paul ends with a solemn confession that nothing can separate us from the love of God revealed in Christ Jesus our Lord.

The paragraph which includes the verses in which we are especially interested (8. 26–27) has a tighter structure than the other two which with it make up the body of the chapter. 8. 18 states not so much a subject to be developed as a *theologoumenon* intended as the foundation of and justification for the rest of the passage; in 8. 19–22 the whole of creation groans and suffers while it waits for the revealing of the sons of God, and in 8. 23–25 we ourselves groan as we wait for the redemption of our bodies. In 8.26–27 the Spirit intercedes for us, and 8. 28–30 form the conclusion of the paragraph.

The three smaller units which we have distinguished are linked by a gradation marked, not only by the increasing importance of the subjects (creation, "we ourselves", the Spirit), of which the same predicate is affirmed or whose actions are qualified in terms drawn from the same predicate (groaning, groan), but also by the phrases which introduce the second and third units. The crescendo appears to be more strongly marked between the first and second units: "*not only* creation, *but (also)* we ourselves, who have the first fruits of the Spirit, groan...*".* Not only does creation, which was subjected to futility, not of its own will but by the will of him who subjected it, groan, but we ourselves, who have the first fruits of the Spirit, who are already a new creation in Christ, also groan.... From alienated creation, which groans "until now", to the Christian who has already received in the Spirit the pledge of future freedom, the repeated mention of groaning creates not so much an intensification as a contrast. In the gradation the second unit acts as a hinge and prevents misunderstanding of the reference of the adverb which begins the third unit. Our groans are incapable of producing a prayer "according to God" (8. 27 *kata Theon*), and the Spirit intercedes for us with wordless groans.

I do not think it can be felt as straining the text to read it as saying that the Spirit prays not only for us, but, in a sense, in our place. "Materially", the gradation appears as follows: the groans of creation, without reference to the Spirit, the groans of those who have the Spirit and the groans, in the latter, of the Spirit alone. The adverb I have translated "in the same way" in 8. 26 now acquires a plausible meaning. It is true that *hōsautōs* can have the meaning "in addition", "moreover",[2] but this is not very likely here. Curiously, exegetes have shown little interest in defining more exactly the structure of the comparison implied by the use of *hōsautōs*. Does the Spirit help us in the same way as others do, in the weakened sense that he also helps us? The context provides no basis for this interpretation. In my view the adverbial phrase "in the same way" (which is my rendering of the Greek adverb *hōsautōs*) depends on the "not only . . . but also" of 8.23, and means that the relation of resemblance is like this: "We groan . . . and the Spirit helps us in the same way, by groaning."

The contrast which marks the relation between the first two units perhaps indicates that the second unit has a tension within itself which is not resolved until the third unit. The opening of 8. 23 can be expanded in a manner perfectly in harmony with Pauline theology as follows: "because we have the first fruits of the Spirit (the first fruits which is the Spirit), we groan as we wait for the fullness". The movement of the text, however, seems to suggest a concession: "although we already have the Spirit, we still groan". This would make the climax stand out more sharply, and the relation between the second and third units would be one of contrast, just like that between the first and the second: the Spirit, whose presence in us does not prevent our groaning, himself also groans.

We should beware of seeing in the gradation that I have just analysed the expression of an inference based on an experimental knowledge of the subject-matter of the first and second units. The redemption of our bodies is an object of hope, and creation's anguished waiting is an apocalyptic theme, and its function in the Pauline context ought to be examined before it is used as the basis for a complete cosmic eschatology. Paul's starting-point for

[2] To be completely accurate, it is the whole phrase *hōsautōs de kai* which has to be analysed.

this exposition is probably the certainty of the eschatological gift of the Spirit, that saving power which God still keeps hidden in himself with Christ, but which is already active in the "hearts" of men. It is because of this sure hope that the Spirit is the "means" by which God will give life to our mortal bodies that Paul can speak of the groans of those who have been saved in this hope (in the objective sense of the word). And it is the same certainty which allows Paul to use, with magnificent freedom, the apocalyptic image of the birth-pangs coming upon the world as it nears the messianic time or the time of the final consummation. The hope for the redemption of our bodies is a measure of the extent to which our mortal bodies keep us still in solidarity with the world subjected to "futility" and "decay". In "taking the measure" of our present state, Paul uses images which are neither psychological or cosmological. The pattern of the gradation which forms the structure of Rom. 8. 19–27 should be seen as "revealed" or "translated" in the climax of the gradation.

"Our Weakness" (8.26)

The commentators are practically unanimous in understanding these words of our inability to pray to God "properly". This interpretation seems to be supported by a chiastic type of construction:

(a) the Spirit helps us
(b) in our weakness
(b') for we do not know what to ask for to make our prayer a true prayer,
(a') but the Spirit himself intercedes with wordless groans.

On this view the second half of the verse explains the first, but reverses the order of the terms to be explained. I suggest that this interpretation is less probable, or at least no more probable, than another which I wish to put forward. The chiasmus is too formal in its articulation for there to be any strict correspondence between the symmetrical terms, in this case, a correspondence between definienda and definitions. "The Spirit" appears in both (a) and (a'), but "weakness" appears only in (b). Moreover, if it is accepted that "in the same way" in 8. 26 places in relation "we ourselves" (8. 23) and the Spirit in respect of the *tertium com-*

parationis, groaning, then "weakness" deserves attention in its own right. A simple paraphrase will show the consistency of this term in our hypothesis: The Spirit helps us in our weakness in the same way, with (or "in") groans; that is to say, in prayer, when we do not know how to ask "properly", the Spirit intercedes for us, in groans. In other words, if the second part of the verse is an explanation of "in the same way", "weakness" must also receive an exact definition from the previous context.

"Weakness" describes the existential situation of those who have been given up to the sufferings of the present time (8. 18) and still wait for God to set their mortal bodies free from "decay". Paul uses the term and related terms in the plural, with a reference to the trials of apostolic activity. Deeper than the existential situation, what is described by "weakness" is vulnerability to sin and scandal, even in the baptized, and a sort of internal limit which is a sort of anticipated presence of death. In the baptized, however, weakness takes on a different meaning; it becomes the chosen site, to the scandal of the Jews and ridicule of the Greeks, of the operation of the saving power which is the Spirit of God. For those who hope, weakness thus understood is evidence that they are, as it were, suffering the birthpangs of glory.

It is in this weakness, in my view, that the Spirit helps us, and not directly and formally in the inability which weighs on our desire to pray. Since this weakness affects even prayer, through which we want to express to God our aspiration to be delivered from it[3]—because prayer remains tied to "decay"—it is in prayer that the Spirit comes to our assistance. The reduction of this powerlessness to something passing—even if experienced by all the baptized—or the connection of "properly", against all linguistic probability, with "we do not know" both weaken the passage. In a text in which Paul proclaims the certainty which dwells in Christian hope in the midst of the sufferings of the present time, an assertion of a weakness with no qualification, no connection with particular conditions or circumstances, has a

[3] "Aspiration" translates the Greek *phronēma*, which can mean both "behaviour" and "intention". In Paul the term (which is used four times in Romans) stands for what occupies the mind of someone who is directed to a specific end and aspires to reach it.

universal and fundamental bearing: we are incapable of praying "according to the will of God". This is as irreducib'e an inability as the need to prayer is permanent. Nor is there anything to suggest that the Spirit pours into us the prayer which is pleasing to God. Weakness reaches a point here which is beyond the realm in which the Christian can take over Paul's exclamation, "When I am weak, then I am strong" (2 Cor. 12. 10). In contrast, the Christian in prayer confesses: I am weak, and the Spirit makes up for my weakness, not even by his power, but with groans.

The Intercession of the Spirit

The interpretation which apparently best combines respect for the text and the need to explain it by other Pauline texts is the one which has recently been revived and which attributes the groans of the Spirit to the charism of speaking with tongues. Ernst Käsemann gave a new authority to this interpretation a few years ago, and quite recently it has been taken up by H. R. Balz.[4] On the other hand, there is no suggestion of this interpretation in 1 Corinthians 14. The man who speaks in a tongue is like a foreigner to the other members of the assembly, and does nothing to build them up (1 Cor. 14. 11, 12, 17). The charism of interpretation, it is true, whether it is given to the speaker with tongues himself or to another charismatic, allows the assembly to be edified from the speaking in tongues. But if the prayer of the speaker in tongues is translatable, it is necessarily distinguished from the groans of which Paul claims that he who searches hearts knows the desire they express; for according to the most certain witness of the Scriptures and of Judaism the knowledge of him who searches hearts is, in itself, incommunicable and untranslatable. Moreover, 1 Cor. 14. 28 leaves little room for the hypothesis that the charism of tongues allows the assembly both to confess its inability to pray "according to God" and to give

[4] Ernst Käsemann, "Der gottesdienstliche Schrei nach der Freiheit". This article first appeared in 1964 in *Apophoreta* (Festschrift für E. Haenchen), and was reprinted in *Paulinische Perspektiven* (Tübingen, 1969), pp. 211–36.
H. R. Balz, *Heilsvertrauen und Welterfahrung—Strukturen der paulinischen Eschatologie nach Römer 8, 13–39*, Beiträge zur evang. Theol. 59, (Munich, 1971).

thanks for the intercession of the Spirit, signified by unintelligible sounds. There is no indication that speaking in tongues reveals to the assembly intercession by the Spirit on behalf of the saints. Finally, if Rom. 8. 27 does indeed reflect the fact that Paul was thinking in terms of the community, the text has to be forced to provide a reference to the liturgical assembly. In short, the proof that 8. 26 refers to speaking with tongues comes back to the gratuitous assertion, in the face of the contrary implication of 1 Cor. 14. 14, that the only key to its meaning is speaking in tongues.

The Spirit's groans are described by an adjective which can be rendered either "wordless" or "which words cannot express". Both senses are claimed by exegetes who connect 8. 26 with speaking in tongues: "wordless" could apply to inarticulate sounds, unintelligible to the profane, such as speakers in tongues utter, and not of groans not accompanied by words; "which words cannot express" would refer to speaking in tongues which was untranslatable in its extravagance—which would embarrass those who keep room for the charism of interpretation—and not to what provoked groans and so went beyond the possibilities of articulation in concepts and words. If we exclude speaking with tongues as a solution, there are two possible senses. Bauer prefers the first, "wordless", and mentions that this translation has the support of the Syriac and Armenian versions. The choice of the second meaning, for which *arrhētois* (rather than *alalētois*) would be more usual, can claim the support of 8. 27, which seems to oppose the wisdom of God to the weakness of human minds and words, like other Pauline texts on the transcendence of the eschatological gifts, which are in fact the object of the Spirit's aspiration. Nevertheless, 8. 27 can equally well mean that God hears the Spirit's groans, but we cannot grasp them precisely because they are wordless. Since the Spirit's groans are meant, not to cure our inability to ask "according to God", for God's own gifts, but to make up for it, the adjective "wordless" must mean that the Spirit's intercession is quite different from our prayer: the Spirit has no need of our words to make himself understood by God.

St Paul ascribes to the Spirit intercession on behalf of the saints. In view of the saying in Rom. 8. 34 that Christ is "at the right hand of God,... indeed intercedes for us", it is tempting to bring in the figure of the Paraclete, whose characteristics are given in the Johannine writings both to Christ and to the Spirit. The tradition of the Paraclete as helper, representative and inter-cessor—the senses of consoler and defender must be excluded from the New Testament, except perhaps for the latter in 1 Jn. 2. 1—would then underlie the passage we are considering. It should be noticed, however, that in the present state of the sources this passage is the only place where there is a mention of the Paraclete's groaning, if indeed we are to identify Spirit and Paraclete in these verses. On the premiss that the Intercessor is a heavenly figure (Rom. 8. 34; cf. Heb. 7. 25), some exegetes have thought that the intercession of Rom. 8. 26–27 is a heavenly, apocalyptic (O. Michel) "event" of priestly mediation (J. Schneider).[5]

In my view, however, these exegetes neglect an important point in our text, namely, that God, who knows what the Spirit's aspiration is, is called "he who searches hearts". This is of course a formula, but not so fixed that its elements lose their individual meaning. This gives us a justification for saying that it is in the hearts of the baptized that God looks for and hears the aspiration of the Spirit. We may recall that our "hearts" have received the gift of the Spirit (Rom. 5. 5) and the gift of the Spirit as guar-antee (2 Cor. 1. 22), and that the Spirit has been sent into our hearts (Gal. 4. 6). This idea of the heart as the place of God's action first appears in the great prophecies of Jeremiah and Ekeziel on the renewal of man's heart (Jer. 31. 31–34; Ezek. 11. 14–21).

In this light the intercession of the Spirit appears as the help of a messenger who is with us and in us. It is only this "condition" of the Spirit living in us which creates the possibility of his groan-ing. The Spirit is given to us as the guarantee of our inheritance; as such, he aspires in us, in us he is an aspiration to the fullness and the glory which God holds in reserve for those whom he loves. He alone can intercede "according to God", according to

[5] O. Michel, *Der Brief an die Römer*, Kritisch-exegetisches Kommentar über das NT, 4 (Göttingen, [4]1966), p. 208.

J. Schneider, "*Stenazō*", *Theologisches Wörterbuch zum NT*, 7, p. 602, n. 12.

God's purpose of making many brethren conformed to the image of his Son. We "know" that, for those who love God, all things, and especially the sufferings of the present time, are "preparing" a weight of glory beyond comparison (2 Cor. 4. 17). We know this and believe it, and this knowledge and belief live in our hope. But how can the prayer of a being which is still "weak" measure up to the glory which will eliminate all weakness? The power of salvation is working in our weakness, and even through it, but it cannot, without taking it out of the present time, produce from it an aspiration which measures up to salvation itself. Only the Spirit as the pledge, the first fruits of glory, as the principle of rebirth in glory, can form such an aspiration in us. The Spirit groans in us, not because he aspires to our liberation from the sufferings of the present time, but because these sufferings are a sign that glory is near, and give him the means of bringing glory to birth in us, of being himself the birth of glory in us.

We may add, to conclude these exegetical remarks, that the Spirit intercedes on behalf of "the saints", that is to say, the Christian community, whether or not it is meeting for a liturgical celebration. Christian prayer, especially when it is an aspiration to salvation—which, ultimately, it always is—is a prayer which goes up from the heart of the community, involves the community and expresses and strengthens the unity of its hope. This prayer is a confession of inability to pray in a way that is pleasing to God and the certainty that the Spirit who has been given to us intercedes for us at our very aspiration to the glory in which we shall share a single inheritance.

The Importance of Rom. 8. 26–27 for the Theology of Prayer

I do not believe that there is a contradiction between Paul's personal prayer and his invitations to the recipients of his letters to pray without ceasing, to offer petitions and supplications to God, on the one hand, and the unique assertion of Rom. 8. 26 on the other, that we do not know what we should ask for so as to be in conformity with God's plan of salvation. There are two distinct levels. The first is the level of the many demands which can only be, in the last resort, the manifold desire that the will of God be done, that in all things man should be led by grace to believe in deed and in truth that our actions already

carry in them the glory which is to come. In fact we do not ask
for anything. Knowing that without the other side of death
established by the resurrection of Christ, without the Spirit who
comes to us from that other side, life lacks meaning and value,
we confess our complete weakness through the many confessions
of our varied and repeated weaknesses and of our needs and wishes
and we cry out our hope. We do not ask to be delivered from
the sufferings of the present time, but ask for faith and light to
see in them the nearness, the already powerful presence of the
Kingdom.

There is also the second fundamental level of the request for
salvation, or, rather, the request that there may be given to us in
its fullness the gift of salvation we have already obtained in
Christ. This request, as we have just suggested, includes all the
others, is implied and active in them. We know the object it
aspires to receive, but we are incapable of making it measure up
to him who keeps in reserve for his own the blessings of the
Kingdom. To claim that we were capable of doing this, even by
the pure grace of God, would be equal to telling God his own
plan, the "purpose" mentioned in Rom. 8. 28–30. The weakness
of 8. 26 characterizes the present state of the Christian who is
still in the flesh. To this weakness there corresponds, not a general inability to pray, but an inability to form what might be
called the primordial prayer. The help which the Spirit gives us
in our weakness consists in making up for this inability, not re-
moving it, by his secret but sure intercession. The heart of our
prayer and of our hope is this certainty, that God has not put his
Spirit into our hearts as a pledge without being aware that the
Spirit calls forth the full gift: God knows what is the aspiration
of the Spirit.

In the light of this theological position I would like now to
make a few remarks on various questions to do with the forms
and practice of prayer. If the interpretation I have put forward
of Rom. 8. 26–27 is correct, what does it tell us about the practice of prayer? Does it justify, for example, a form of mysticism,
a mysticism of silent prayer? We should say from the start that
the intercession of the Spirit cannot be localized: it does not produce any particular prayer. To want to experience the intercession of the Spirit or to be aware of it (and these are very

dubious terms) is to want to transcend the weakness of the flesh and anticipate the revelation of the sons of God. This does not mean, however, that a mystical prayer cannot be based on the intercession of the Spirit, which is at the same time incommunicable to the baptized and the hidden heart of his prayer. Taking up a suggestion made by K. Niederwimmer,[6] we may ask whether the prayer of the speaker with tongues was perhaps a sort of echo of the intercession of the Spirit, not expressing it or translating it but giving expression to the feelings which the guarantee of eternal life aroused in his hope. In our own time the Spirit can raise up similar and quite different charisms in the Church, and by so doing show that his intercession has come to the aid of our weakness.

In my view, however, the truest mysticism, if that word can still be used, is a sort of spirituality immanent in all prayer, a spirituality of humility and poverty in the confession of our utter inability to form a prayer worthy of God and of what he is preparing for his own. It is a spirituality of absolute confidence based on the certainty that there lives within us an intercessor whom God hears and who is the guarantee of our inheritance as sons of God, a spirituality which, far from discouraging petition, frees it from anguish, doubt and the need to possess and makes it a path which leads us through the trials of the present time to the certainty that nothing can separate us from the love of God in Christ Jesus our Lord.

Such a spirituality entails certain rules. Prayer should be sober. Some modern prayers seem to dictate to God, not only what he should do, but the means he should use to do the will we ascribe to him. Other prayers are less requests than celebrations of man and his activity, or encouragements to oneself to change the world. In the eyes of faith, however, our actions have their final counterpart, the final revelation of their meaning, only in a glory still hidden which the people of God is called to share one day, not the glory of transforming the world into a worthy and lasting dwelling-place for the rule of God. If Christians pray, it is because they believe that their acts receive their final meaning on the other side of death. In prayer Christians put aside their pre-

[6] "Das Gebet des Geistes, Rom. 8. 26 f.", *Theol. Zeitschrift* 20 (1964), p. 263.

tensions to possess life, to have it completely mapped out, to have defined its final meaning. Praying is blessing God for the absolute kindness with which he calls us to become a new creation in Christ and a confession of our utter powerlessness "properly" to desire the accomplishment of God's will. Our many requests give that prayer the body it needs to bring about our surrender to God.

Invocation of God under the name of Father acquires its true meaning in prayer thus understood. When we cry out, "Abba, Father!" we are confessing, in the form of an invocation, that, being found in Christ by the mercy of God, we have access to the Father of him who was established Son of God in power. To recognize God as Father means to believe that we are not meant for death, but, pardoned and saved, are destined one day to be made completely alive in and through the Son. But, paradoxically, the primordial prayer of sons is impossible for us. We have received the guarantee of the Spirit and know that we are incapable of inserting, as it were, our prayer in between that guarantee and the total happiness of which it is the pledge. Between the invocation of God as Father and the intercession of the Spirit at the heart of our weakness there enter the tension of a hope waiting for its fulfilment and the paradox of a prayer all the freer and more confident because it knows itself to be indwelt in its very weakness by the one whose groans are heard by God.

Translated by Francis McDonagh

Patrick Jacquemont

Is Action Prayer?

THE title given us for this article on prayer seems to us to reflect a real problem facing Christians, and at the same time to be symptomatic of a complex of problems within which they ask this question.

It is obvious first of all that the Christian who takes his presence in the world and his participation in men's struggles seriously must ask himself about the place that prayer can occupy in his life. The question is not a new one; it was asked by Martha in the gospel (Luke 9. 38–48) with reference to Mary. But for the last twenty years it has been much more acute. Young people and active, militant Catholics have been devoting themselves to urgent political tasks with much energetic faith and hope that they are often no longer able to see clearly what prayer can mean. A large number of them give up prayer, either deliberately or with a bad conscience. Some try to rescue prayer by expecting it to nourish the dynamism of their action, or by identifying prayer with action. It is not certain whether either group gets anything from this. At the same time, when there are signs, paradoxically, of a return to prayer, either vindicated in the name of tradition or rediscovered as it flares up in a more charismatic form, the issue of human commitment and political choice cannot be avoided. In France, Taizé has concerned itself with the problems of the Third World, while in the case of other movements and communities, their attitudes or implicit choices with regard to social and political life have been called into question. It is impossible to avoid the relationship between prayer and action.

But to express this issue in terms of prayer and action is to pose it in the context of a whole set of unanswered questions. It is to assume that prayer and action are in fact distinct from one another, even though one may be ready to recognize that there are activities of prayer or that action can be drawn into prayer. Is it sufficient to say "prayer is at the heart of action" and that "earthly action is the body of prayer"[1] to resolve in this unity a problem still stated in dualist terms? Must we instead recognize and vindicate the autonomy and the specific nature of prayer with regard to other human activities? One may ask whether it would not be preferable to try to pose the question in different terms. Perhaps we should refuse to restrict Christian prayer to the choice between action and prayer, which overlaps in fact with the antithesis between action and contemplation. Perhaps we should also accept that what we should look for is not so much the specific nature of the activity of prayer, as what is original in Christian prayer. In this way it should be possible to distinguish the diverse activities of Christian life without treating them as opposed to each other. When they are reduced to their proper rank of intermediaries, the activities necessary for a life of prayer no longer take the place of the life of prayer itself, which from then on is able to blow like a breath through the whole of existence.

I. Prayer and Life

When we speak of the problems of prayer and action, we must recognize behind these terms two other terms which in fact condition the whole complex of questions. If action and prayer are inevitably presented in a situation of conflict, this is because those who so present them are inevitably thinking of the contrast between action and contemplation. One cannot make any progress

---

[1] I have taken these from P.-Y. Emery's *La prière au cœur de la vie*, Les Presses de Taizé, pp. 39–85. This is the most interesting recent study of our subject, together with that by J.-P. Jossua, "La foi comme dépassement de la tension entre l'action et la prière", *Rev. Sc. Ph. Th.* 56 (1972), pp. 241–51. One may also consult "Prière et action", *Lumen Vitae* 24 (1969). I have sketched out a preliminary approach to this theme in one chapter of my book *Oser prier* (Paris, 1969), pp. 55–64. See also F. Bertrand and G. Bessière, *Prière de profanes* (Paris, 1968).

in the discussion of the relationship between action and prayer without rejecting the dividing line spontaneously drawn between prayer and contemplation. We must reconsider the totalitarianism of a concept of contemplation which is held to express the essence of the nature of prayer. This seems all the more necessary in that this attitude provokes an equally totalitarian view of action which itself no longer permits an understanding of the possible links between prayer and action.

1. *From the Vision of God to Life*

Before entering into a critical analysis of the vocabulary of contemplation applied to Christian prayer, let us make it quite clear that we are not calling into question the profound experience of "contemplatives", both in monasteries and in the world. The very truth of a contemplative life makes it necessary to find complements and correctives for what would otherwise be no more than "contemplation" in the strict sense. The life and action of the Spirit always breaks through concepts. But we see this as yet another reason for overcoming the ambiguous way of presenting Christian prayer as contemplation.

It would be impossible to discuss here how Christian prayer was gradually taken over by contemplation. The reader who is interested should consult the article in the *Dictionnaire de Spiritualité* on this word.[2] One cannot but be astonished to see what the Bible says about seeking for God and about prayer discussed under the heading of "Contemplation". The contradiction is a striking one in the case of the Old Testament, which repeatedly reminds us that "man shall not see God and live" (Exod. 33. 20), and which certainly stresses listening to God much more than seeing God. It is often forgotten too, that the term contemplation is used only once in the New Testament, and then in a very

---

[2] *Dictionnaire de Spiritualité* II/2 (Paris, 1953), cols. 1643–2193. We need hardly state that the 550 columns of this article are indispensable to the study of contemplation and Christian prayer. My critical analysis merely sets out to show what is revealed by certain choices made by the writers.

For a more limited study of the relationship between action and contemplation, see P. T. Camelot, "Action et contemplation dans la tradition chrétienne", *La Vie Spirituelle* 78 (1948), pp. 272–301, and *Initiation théologique* III (Paris, 1952), pp. 1110–46.

ordinary sense.[3] And what are we to say when the question of
action or contemplation is applied to the life of Jesus himself?
We do not deny the importance of seeking a vision of God in
Scripture, and particularly of the use by St John of the verb
"contemplate" (*theorein*) to speak of the knowledge of faith
(e.g., John 6. 40). But can one speak of a specific activity of
knowledge, or even more of a state of life, in the way in which
Christians were later to speak of the contemplative life and the
active life to distinguish the life of prayer and the life of works?

This distinction, which is not found in Scripture, was on the
other hand familiar to the Greeks, from whom it was borrowed.
They drew a contrast between the active life (*bios praktikos*) i.e.,
the life of the man involved in the affairs of this world, and the
contemplative, "theoretic" life (*bios theoretikos*) of the wise man
set free from all the restrictions of this life. Philo, and then the
Church Fathers of the Alexandrian school, first introduced this
distinction into the Christian tradition, and Augustine and Maxi-
mus the Confessor were the great advocates of it.[4] It would be
ridiculous to neglect this important aspect of the Church's
spiritual life. One could in fact show how theologians have tried
to find a proper Christian balance in this dualism, so dear to
Greek thought from Plato to Plotinus. But one might equally
ask whether it might have been more useful if they had tried to
go beyond this dualism, for it always brought with it the risk
of separating prayer from life, and of restricting prayer to certain privileged times or persons.

Irenaeus of Lyons seems to have taken this step. He did not
minimize man's longing to see God. For him "the glory of God
is the living man", but he adds, "but the life of man is the vision
of God". We must understand, however, that what Irenaeus meant
by the vision of God was the communication of the very life of
God. "For if the revelation of God by creation gives life to all
who live on earth, how much more will the manifestation of the
Father by the Word give life to those who see God."[5] This brings
us back from the vision of God to life. The vision of God breaks

[3] The word "contemplation" (*theōria*) is found only once in the New
Testament, in Luke 23. 48, in the trivial sense of the sight that one sees.
[4] *Op. cit.*, cols. 1681–3.
[5] *Contra haereses* IV.20.7. (*Sources chrétiennes* 100, 2nd edn., Paris, p. 649.)

out of the limits that may lie in the metaphor of "vision" itself. Does this not bring us to what is most essential in the Christian revelation about man's approach to God and about prayer? For he whom we desire to meet or be united with breaks the bounds of the intermediaries which we have chosen for this purpose. No doubt these intermediaries must be allowed to play their full role, for without them there is no real human life; but the fact that they ultimately fall away is an invitation to us to treat each of them as relative. Thus we cannot agree that prayer should be reduced to the particular act of seeing God or contemplating him, when in fact it is far wider and more profound, extending to the very life that man leads with God.

2. *From Practice to Life*

Contemplation, then, ought not to be regarded as the privileged basis of Christian prayer, but nor should action. In a civilization which seeks to exalt action, prayer must not become the worship of Prometheus.[6] This is a serious temptation for Christians who find prayer difficult and "contemplative" kinds of prayer discredited. "In the beginning was the Word" invites us to listen. "In the beginning was the Light" awakens a desire for knowledge. The modern world has chosen for the first words of its testament the words of Goethe: "In the beginning was the Act." Must prayer be defined as "action" in order to be recognized as an activity worthy of technological man?

We shall not discuss at length the oversimplification which identifies prayer with action: "To work is to pray." Work, like every other reality of human life, can be pervaded by prayer. But to say that an action is prayer, it is necessary to define the sense in which we talk of Christian prayer. Similarly, prayer cannot be reduced to an activity measured in terms of efficiency, and programmed like a production process aiming at a particular result. We must mistrust that kind of recovery of prayer by

---

[6] We take "Prometheus" here as the myth widely understood as expressing the aim of modern Western man applying his technology and his reason to organize his existence in the context of secularization. We do not claim to pass judgment on the legitimacy of such an interpretation of the mythological figure (cf. the research of Karl Reinhardt, *Eschyle-Euripide*, French trans. by E. Martineau, Coll. "Arguments", Paris, 1972).

men of action who expect it simply to give a new impetus to their work. It is perhaps ambiguous to talk of the gratuitousness of prayer, for while on God's side prayer is a freely given grace, is there not always on the human side a need, a desire or a pleasure? But one can refuse to talk of prayer in terms of usefulness, effectiveness and the return it brings, just as in the end one can refuse to speak of human life in these terms.

It seems to us that the prayer which breaks through the limitations of contemplation also casts doubts on the totalitarianism of action. It is enough to criticize the caricature of action that we know as activism, the disease of a self-devouring activity or of an anguish which seeks this way of running away from itself. Prometheus may have been despised in the world of the sages and the philosophers, but the present-day world may be making an idol of Prometheus. Contemporary man thinks that he is master of his fate, and that he creates himself by his action. "Practice has for so long been raised to an increasingly exalted level that it has now become a tyrant in every sphere of human experience."[7] The religious sphere has not escaped it (religious "practice", Catholic "action"), nor has that of aesthetics (literary "production") nor that of thought (theoretical "practice" or the "production" of concepts).[8]

It is difficult to condemn this "pan-praxism"—we know only too well how this condemnation would be used to divert man from his personal and political responsibilities. The fact remains that one cannot expect action alone to reveal to us everything that man is. Although action must be supreme in its own field, that of technology, morality and politics, it is impossible to understand the totality of human experience on the basis purely of action. In its own way the Gospel points in this direction with the episode of Martha and Mary receiving Jesus, as soon as it is seen outside the context of the contrast between the active and the contemplative life. It is quite clear that Jesus is not reproaching Martha for her care in preparing a meal which does in fact call for work. But Martha is totally involved in the service she

---

[7] B. Quelquejeu, "La lassitude de Prométhée", *Parole et Mission* 55 (1971), p. 117. I am greatly indebted to Quelquejeu in my article.

[8] The allusion is to the work of Louis Althusser: *Pour Marx* (Paris, 1966); *Lire Le Capital*, I and II, in collaboration (Paris, 1966); *Lénine et la philosophie* (Paris, 1969).

is giving. She exists only for this concern, which turns her in upon herself when she wants to offer something to her guest. The attitude of Mary shows us that meaningful action cannot be self-sufficient. Service to others becomes meaningful through the other person who is the guest and who gives Martha the ability to serve. The source and meaning of our action is derived from Another, and there is a totalitarianism of action which makes us forget or ignore this. We must neither contrast Martha and Mary, nor regard Mary as the more privileged, but remember that what gives them life can be reduced neither to action nor to contemplation.

Here again, then, we find life itself as the best possible basis of prayer and for what can be said about it. It is perhaps rather too indeterminate, but it is precisely because it is open in this way that the notion of life seems to us to be able to express what prayer is, and particularly what Christian prayer is.

II. The Prayer of Life

It is, however, not enough to discuss prayer simply on the basis of human experience. We must also take into account what Christian tradition and the New Testament in particular tell us firstly about the prayer of Jesus and secondly about the prayer of Christians.

1. *The Prayer of Jesus is his Life*

In trying to gather together the testimony of the gospels about the prayer of Jesus, there is a risk of overlooking everything except what we are told about Jesus' prayer activities. Jesus took part in the prayer of his people and must have learnt this prayer with Mary and Joseph, in the synagogue and in the temple itself.[9] We must not neglect this community aspect of Jesus' prayer, even though the evangelists found it necessary to emphasize in particular the criticisms which Jesus made of the prayer of the Pharisees (Luke 18. 9–14), the places of worship (John 4. 21) and the temple itself (John 2. 13–21). Luke emphasized the personal prayer of Jesus. Jesus withdrew alone to pray (Luke 5. 16; 6. 12), for example when he found the crowds too

[9] See Aron, *Ainsi priait Jésus enfant* (Paris, 1968).

much for him or just before he chose the apostles. This prayer took place in solitude, in the silence of the night or on the mountain. It is tempting to find in this a justification for a "contemplative life", based on the pattern of Christ withdrawing to pray. There is no question that the evangelist meant to emphasize the times when Christ prayed, to show that he was a man of prayer.

But in order to understand the stress that Luke laid on Jesus' prayer and the meaning that he wanted to give it, we must note how he described Jesus' praying at the time of his baptism (Luke 3. 21–22) and at the transfiguration on the mountain, where he had gone up with Peter, James and John "to pray" (Luke 9. 28). These two episodes show us what Jesus' prayer was. At the Jordan, Jesus, as he prayed, saw the Spirit descending upon him, and a voice was heard saying "Thou art my beloved Son." We must note the role of the Spirit, but must pay particular attention to the voice which shows Jesus listening as a Son. The prayer of Jesus, then, consisted in listening confidently and lovingly to the Father. The same is true of the Transfiguration. Other texts in John show that Jesus was in dialogue with his Father at every moment of his life, and not only in the exceptional moments when the veil was lifted, as at his baptism or at the Transfiguration. All of Jesus' life was lived in relation to his Father: "The Son can do nothing of his own accord, but only what he sees the Father do" (John 5. 19); "As the living Father sent me, and I live because of the Father . . ." (John 6. 57). At any moment this profound communion between the Father and the Son could be expressed in explicit prayer. This might be as the result of a thrill of joy which evoked a blessing of God in the midst of the crowd (Matt. 11. 25–27) or of the disciples (Luke 10. 21–22). It might take the form of a meditation shared with others, as at the Last Supper: "I am in the Father and the Father in me" (John 14. 11). "As thou, Father, art in me, and I in thee, that they also may be one in us" (John 17. 21). At the hour of his testing the fear of being abandoned still took the form of a prayer addressed to the Father (Matt. 27. 46). Or else his confidence as a Son was expressed in his prayer at the very moment of temptation: "Not as I will, but as thou wilt" (Matt. 26. 39).

Here we have the mark of the prayer of Jesus and the secret which gives it life. "My food is to do the will of him who sent

me" (John 4. 34). The author of the letter to the Hebrews expressed the nature of the prayer of Jesus, which was inseparable
from his life itself (Heb. 10. 5–7), very well: "Consequently, when
Christ came into the world, he said, 'Sacrifices and offerings
thou hast not desired, but a body hast thou prepared for me; in
burnt offerings and sin offerings thou hast taken no pleasure.
Then I said, "Lo, I have come to do thy will, O God", as it is
written of me in the roll of the book.' " The prayer which is
acceptable to God is that of Christ, because it is the offering of
a whole life which carries out the will of the Father in confidence
and communion. The times when Jesus prayed explicitly should
not be seen in isolation, even if they point to the place of prayer
in his life. The prayer of Jesus is his whole life.

2. *The Life of a Christian is his Prayer*

If Jesus' prayer is the offering of his life, surely the prayer of
the Christian is no less? Paul helps us to look in the direction
that Jesus followed. How could he call upon us to pray constantly (1 Thess. 5. 17) if he had not said that the spiritual sacrifice of the Christian is the offering of his life: "I appeal to you
therefore, brethren, by the mercies of God, to present your bodies
as a living sacrifice, holy and acceptable to God, which is your
spiritual worship" (Rom. 12. 1)?

The prayer of the Christian is prayer "in spirit and truth",
as Jesus told the Samaritan woman (John 4. 24). Thus we should
not begin to describe prayer by defining where and when it takes
place, but rather by recognizing that it is the Spirit who breathes
life into a Christian's prayer. If the Christian is to make his own
the prayer which Jesus addressed to his Father, he must have
the help of the Spirit: "The Spirit helps us in our weakness; for
we do not know how to pray as we ought" (Rom. 8. 26) and we
have received the Spirit of adopted sons which makes us cry
"Abba! Father!" (Rom. 8. 15). Like the prayer of Christ, the
prayer of the Christian is a confident and constant dialogue between Son and Father, animated by the Spirit.

Now Paul shows us that the gift of the Spirit enters the whole
of our life, and not only certain aspects of it. Discussing fornication, he reminds Christians that their very bodies are temples of
the Holy Spirit (1 Cor. 6. 19). Consequently, the Christian prays

with his body, which does not simply mean that his body must be associated with the expression of the prayer, but that the life of the body can glorify God: "So glorify God in your body." What applies to the body applies to all its activities. The Christian must do everything for the glory of God: "So, whether you eat or drink, or whatever you do, do all to the glory of God" (1 Cor. 10. 31) and "Whatever you do, in word or deed, do everything in the name of the Lord Jesus, giving thanks to God the Father through him" (Col. 3. 17). The true Christian worship is a spiritual worship which inspires the whole of life, when this life is full of the Spirit (1 Cor. 3. 16), when the life of the Christian is the life of Jesus who lives in him (Gal. 2. 20). In this sense, we can reply in a positive sense to the question which our article poses—Yes, we can reply, action can be prayer, if the action is animated by the Spirit which makes it a living sacrifice to the Father.

In these circumstances, we can allow Paul's call to pray without ceasing to have its full meaning. Not only does the Christian know that "in everything" (Phil. 4. 6) he may have recourse to prayer. In fact God is not a stranger to any of the realities of human life, for he created men. But "in all circumstances" (1 Thess. 5. 18) the Christian can give thanks, for the Son has taken on his human condition in order to transfigure it. And "always and for everything" (Eph. 5. 20), the Christian must pray in the Spirit, for the breath of God never ceases to be active: "Pray at all times in the Spirit" (Eph. 6. 18). The life of the Christian, animated by the Spirit of Jesus, can be prayer at all times.

III. The Life of Prayer

The Christian's prayer is the worship of the whole of his life, but there are also specific activities of this prayer which prepare for it, which make it present or which prolong it. These activities are not primary—the action of the Spirit is primary in Christian prayer. They are, however, indispensable intermediaries for man. In fact it is because man has a dignity created by God that he can firstly prepare himself for prayer, secondly become aware of it, and thirdly extend prayer into life. These are the conditions of Christian prayer.

1. *Preparations*

To prepare himself for prayer, man needs to control his body and mind and to be calm and concentrated. No wise man would ever neglect to prepare himself in this way for profound meditation, and the Christian at prayer can profit greatly from this attitude in order to listen to the breathing of the Spirit and to receive the Word. Everything that helps the Christian to attend in this way to the inspired Word will similarly help him to welcome the Spirit, whose activity transforms the meditation of the wise man into the prayer of the Christian.

But the Spirit will also find fertile soil in the life of the Christian who is actively committed to the struggle for justice, freedom and peace. The asceticism of militancy is different from that of meditation, but it too requires a concentration of effort, which will enable the active Christian to transform his energy into the love and service of others. The same can be said of the creative craft of the artist, who, because of his own kind of asceticism, can change the creative act into prayer. Man is most human not only in his inner life but also in his outward expression. He may bury himself in the one or lose himself in the other. But both can be filled by the Spirit, who thereby makes what began as preparation a true prayer offered to the Father.

2. *Self-awareness*

Christian prayer is not only prepared for by the human activities of meditation, militancy and creativity. It also seeks to become aware of itself in a specific activity, to identify itself and to make itself known to others. Christian prayer is self-awareness and self-expression.

Self-awareness in prayer is usually thought of as an attitude of recollectedness, but what it really means is welcoming the Spirit in secrecy and silence. "But when you pray, go into your room and shut the door and pray to your Father who is in secret" (Matt. 6. 6). The life of prayer needs this experience of withdrawal and rumination. Let us not forget, however, that if Christian prayer is described as secret, this is not so much because it is silent and solitary, but because it is concealed from the eyes of men and, what is more, intangible even to the person who prays, for it is a prayer which does not know itself and remains in the secret of God who alone knows it.[10]

This self-awareness ought to be sought in the prayer of the Christian community. Christ is present in the community because it is gathered together in his name. The Spirit of Christ invoked in the epiclesis transforms the prayer of the faithful who are offering their lives and confessing their faith in prayer, for the true expression of faith is always doxology. It is in the community that the prayer of the Christian is embodied, and he becomes aware what Christian prayer is in the midst of his brethren who are worshipping together. It is there that the meaning and the living breath of prayer are imparted to him; it is there that in his turn he can express and bear witness to it. Christian prayer needs the liturgical celebration of the community to become conscious of what it is.[11]

3. Extensions

If prayer is prepared for by particular actions and achieves self-awareness in the specific activities of the life of the Christian, it is extended in that life itself, which it enables to evolve, or draw into the fire and the force of the Spirit.

If prayer is thought of as quite separate from ordinary life, the inevitable corollary is that the Christian has to return or to be sent back to everyday life. But the extension of the prayer of life is quite different from this. The Christian who offers the whole of his life to be transmuted by the fire of the Spirit does not need to return to life after praying. On the contrary, his life is returned to him renewed. If he becomes aware that the Spirit is praying in his life, he will eventually understand what the Spirit is making of this life and even experience the fruits of the Spirit in his life. We do not speak enough of the fruits of the Spirit as the flowering of life, as song, praise and prayer. When Paul calls us to a life of constant prayer in thanksgiving, he does so after recalling the fruits born in the life of the Christian—peace, joy (1 Thess. 5. 13, 16, 17), forbearance (Ph. 4. 4, 5, 6) and the fullness of the Spirit (Eph. 5. 18, 20). The fruits of the Spirit

[10] See my article "La Prière qui s'ignore", *Christus* 68 (1970), pp. 445-9.
[11] See my article "Prière chrétienne et communauté", *Cahiers Saint-Dominique* 124 (1971-1972), pp. 198-204.

are the prayer of thanksgiving. It is this that gives prayer its true flavour and makes it possible to enjoy it. This enjoyment of prayer is not restricted to a pious minority or to moments of collective exaltation. It is a fruit of the Spirit which causes the life of prayer to flourish in peace and happiness.

This way of looking at prayer must not be thought too enthusiastic, for the Christian who seeks prayer in his life comes to see too how the Spirit is praying the groaning of a creation which is looking forward to salvation (Rom. 8. 26, 22). The awareness in prayer of the work of the Spirit in the world binds the person who is praying more closely to the human activities of the transformation of the universe, where the groaning of the Spirit can be perceived. When the prayer of life cannot be thanksgiving, it can still be an active demand for participation in the creative activity of God. Christian prayer does not withdraw a person from life, but helps him to set life free and to take part in God's plan of salvation.

Christian prayer is therefore not separate from life. No doubt silent meditation and the celebration of the community are distinct from other specific human activities, such as work or play. But they are the activities of the same living being, and are inspired by the same living breath of the Spirit. It is the same Spirit which gives man his breath, and makes his breathing prayer.

Translated by R. A. Wilson

Ladislaus Boros

Prerequisites for Christian Prayer

GOD is saying less. I do not mean by this that he does not intervene decisively in the confusion of our time. Not to do so would
hardly accord with God's way of acting. But we are all aware of
something that we find rather extraordinary: God sees, hears and
knows everything, and yet he says nothing.

All those pious men who out of devotion and in the course of
humdrum lives do innumerable good works would dearly like
to hear his voice just once—acknowledging their acts of good-
ness and encouraging his faithful followers. Yet God says nothing. People in the midst of their wrecked lives cry out to him
in all their loneliness, asking for help in their misery. And God
often shows them no sign of his presence, but stays silent.
Throughout the Old Testament we hear the cry of the heavy-
laden: "Unto thee will I cry, O Lord my rock; be not silent to me:
lest, if thou be silent to me, I become like them that go down
into the pit" (Ps. 28. 1). Or: "This thou hast seen, O Lord: keep
not silence: O Lord, be not far from me" (Ps. 35. 22). There are
many more such instances.

And one day the Son of God stood before his enemies. They
accused him, condemned him and abused him. And God said
nothing. Christ prayed aloud on the cross. His heart-rending cry
was a sign of anxiety: "My God, my God, why hast thou forsaken
me?" (Mk. 15. 34). Even then God said nothing. The fact of
God's silence is nothing new. It just seems more acutely obvious
to us today. Men have to reckon with this mystery more than in
the past. Hence the worrying question of our incapability: Is there

any longer any meaning in talking to a silent God, in praying to him?[1]

Our dismay at the alleged "absence of God", at his incomprehensible silence which we experience with such distress and anguish, in fact only makes us feel something of which we were always aware but did not perhaps take seriously enough into account: that is, that God is unutterably above everything that is apart from him and can be conceived apart from him.[2] This is a problem to which, initially, I offer no answer. It will, I hope, be gradually resolved in the course of these reflections. It is also true that despite God's distressing silence, Christ did not dispense with prayer. However open a Christian may be to the Church and the world, however much good he may do, and however much need he may alleviate, however selfless his devotion in this world, something essential is missing if he is not open to God. Even when the windows of a Christian life are open on every side, his deeds do not shine out; they take on no contours and no solidity; they are not properly visible in all their beauty and luminance.

A Christian's behaviour has these qualities only by virtue of a "light from above"—by devotion to a supramundane power and glory. This is missing if in all his concerns, however far and wide he casts, a Christian is essentially on his own, and everything takes place in a circumscribed area closed to any light from above and without any perspective on what lies above. Then a man cannot properly know to whom he is supposed to bear witness, and to whom he is ultimately directed in the very essence of his being.

After this short reference to the two basic experiences of the silence of God and a Christian's dependence on prayer—I should like to consider the main question: What exactly is this prayer that God for the most part answers only with silence and on which a Christian is nevertheless dependent? My attempted

[1] To supplement this short report I should like to draw attention to Fr Wulf's article, "Vom Verlust und der Neuentdeckung des Gebetes in unserer Zeit", *Geist und Leben* 41 (1968), pp. 407–13.

[2] "Super omnia, quae praeter ipsum sunt et concipi possunt, ineffabiliter excelsus." Conc. Vaticanum I. Constitutio dogmatica "Dei filius" de fide catholica. Cap. L. De Deo rerum omnium creatore. D(S) 3002.

answer will be an outline of the "prerequisites" for Christian prayer:

Astonishment

A person is "astonished" if he happens upon something that until then hadn't really struck him, and which seems unusual, strange and new, and at the meaning and origin of which he can only wonder. Astonishment at things Christian is, however, not just temporary. A Christian's life is never free from astonishment; indeed, his surprise grows to the extent that he becomes more aware of what it really means to be a Christian. If a Christian were really fed up with never being wholly master of his own existence, he would have to stop being a Christian. The miracles in the Bible are put forward as "signs", as "warning signals". For us they are not just an extension of something that happened once in the past, but something essentially new. It is precisely this kind of "alarm" that a Christian should experience in regard to his own existence.

But miracles bring both comfort and help. They are always decisively redemptive changes in the course of the world just as it threatens to engulf a man. Miracles are also promises and indications of a redeemed world, in which there will be no more suffering, no more tears, and no more dying. The miracle of all miracles is essentially and decisively new: it is Christ himself, by whom the Christian is continually confronted and challenged anew. Every man who is lucky enough to be astonished and made to wonder at Christ is unknowledged, an other, alien. How, in the compulsion and necessity of his perspective on Christ, can his life be facile, familiar or comprehensible? Being a Christian is always breathtakingly new; something that must overwhelm a man with astonishment and wonder.[3]

Concern

But a Christian can't just stay in a condition of sheer surprise. When, in the way I have described, God evokes wonder and makes a Christian into a man astonished, he also makes a de-

---

[3] In another context, Karl Barth also cites these qualities. See K. Barth, *Einführung in die evangelische Theologie* (Zürich, 1962).

mand upon him, and requires his concern and commitment. In his initial wonder and surprise, the Christian "acceded to" God. God came upon him, encountered him, and took hold of him. There is now no going back. As this person I am, with this particular character, with these qualities, with my so often stubborn and fearful heart, in my historical situation, I am personally called upon by God. A Christian life is first and foremost the particular, wholly personal existence of the individual Christian. It has to do with his vocation and sanctification, with his joy and his suffering; it is a question of the unique occasion and opportunity of his short life and of his death. Being-a-Christian concerns both the whole man and the most intimate private life. Concern binds the Christian to something not only in his private life but in Christianity and Christendom. Everything in Christendom that has to do with a community life as enjoined by God is inescapably a personal concern of the individual Christian. He is concerned by the decree pronounced over and beyond the Christian community and the Church of God; he is affected by the promise given to that community. Everything that happens or does not happen in the life of the people of God, in this or that way, appropriately or inappropriately, for good or for evil, concerns him. It affects the Christian directly; it is ineluctably his concern. And the whole world, in its present history, is a time for God's grace. Even if everyone else could ignore the fate of modern man—mankind today: Europeans and Africans, Americans and Asians, confined Communists and perhaps even more confined anti-Communists, theists and atheists— the Christian cannot do so, for his lot is that he must and ought to orient himself to God. And this God says Yes to all humankind. The Christian lives in the world of today; he is addressed by this world and his heart is pierced by it. "Now when they [the people] heard this, they were pricked in their heart, and said unto Peter and to the rest of the apostles: 'Men and brethren, what shall we do?' " (Acts 2. 37).[4]

[4] Guardini outlined the qualities of "concern" in two short articles: "Vom Sinn der Schwermut" and "Der Ausgangspunkt der Denkbewegung Sören Kierkegaards". Both articles are to be found in R. Guardini, *Unterscheidung des Christlichen* (Mainz, 1963), pp. 502–33 and 473–501.

Obligation

That inward attitude of the Christian that grows out of "astonishment" and "concern" produces a sphere of existence that might be termed "challenge". It is a wonderful and illuminating thing, but also a difficult and even awesome obligation, to be called to one's duty by God in this way. Already, in the initial condition of astonishment, the whole man was clearly affected. Even "concern" affects his whole existence. Of course there are also "peripheral" truths in revelation, which do not involve a Christian in any such obligation, even though they are not without their own specific value. But what directly and "unconditionally concerns" a Christian is the "fullness of God" and the demand he makes on man.

The Christian has to focus his existence on the "centre of belief" and judge everything from that point. He is not allowed to overlook a single point on the "periphery". But he is also forbidden to construct a "second centre" by orienting things from his own self; he may not direct his longing for piety to details. Only Christ is the focal point and centre of our faith and whoever does not collect together with Christ, scatters. To use one's human life to do both things, to cherish everything even though it seem unimportant, but ultimately to be bound only to the one centre, Christ, is to be a Christian in the most profound and devout sense of the word. Everything else is at best (perhaps well-meaning) piety but ultimately has nothing to do with the core of Christianity. In this quiet reference outwards, which comes only from an honestly lived and often also painfully experienced faith, a Christian can be, ought to be, indeed must be a happy man. He knows what life is about. For him there is a "gradient" of faith and of mastery of life. He knows that he is wrapped in God's favour and clemency, and that he has been chosen by God to offer endless praise in unending happiness. In this process he is (not always superficially but always in his innermost depths) a satisfied man, and therefore one who spreads happiness in the world.[5]

[5] Similar ideas are to be found in Karl Rahner's works, above all in two articles, "Geistliche Abendgespräch über den Schlaf, das Gebet und andere Dinge" and "Priester und Dichter", both in K. Rahner, *Schriften zur Theologie*, III (Einsiedeln and Zürich, 1956), pp. 263–81 and 349–75

Loneliness

The Christian lives in this world (not just "situationally" but essentially) as a solitary. It is not always easy to bear this isolation with dignity and serenity. Being a Christian is certainly not an anti-human but an essentially critical and in fact revolutionary pursuit. Anyone who tries fully to be a Christian has to remember that he belongs to a minority group. This loneliness—if it produces no despondency or irony—can be sustained only by an extreme degree of peacefulness. It is probably true to say that a Christian (precisely when he lives from the very depths of his being-a-Christian) can hardly ever be popular (either among the so-called "children of this world" or among the "pious"). Anyone who takes this being-a-Christian seriously has to survive loneliness in understanding and peace. Paul, who proclaimed the Christian life, emphasized this point. In the second chapter of his First Letter to the Corinthians, he explains what he means by having the "mind of Christ". The "spiritual man", the Christian, is a mystery. The world does not understand him, but he understands the world. This does not mean that he is more gifted, more intelligent, and more independent in character. He can judge the world because he is grounded in the freedom of Christ. This gives him a certain distance from the world, which no one can obtain in the world itself—not even the most gifted of all. It is precisely in this groundedness in Christ that the Christian remains a solitary.[6]

Doubt

This fifth condition for Christian prayer is dangerous: it does not impinge from without, but tends to occur in the very process of prayer itself. No Christian, young or old, pious or not so pious, should forget that for some reason and in some way he is a doubter, and one who is by no means at the end of, or about to dispense with, his doubting. He might just as well doubt that he is a poor sinner and at best one redeemed from the fire. But

(English translations in *Theological Investigations*, vol. 3, London and New York, 1968).

[6] Profit is still to be gained from reading (in regard to loneliness in faith and prayer emanating from this loneliness): P. Lippert, *Der Mensch Job redet mit Gott* (Munich, 1934).

the Christian should not despair because he doubts, even when his doubt is extreme. Above all he ought not to despair, since in the present situation of redemption his doubt belongs essentially to faith, and does so as a condition for the possibility of belief itself. His prayer can never be other than the humble: "I believe, help thou my unbelief" (Mk. 9. 24). Genuine belief can exist only as conquered doubt.[7] For this reason, a Christian ought not to be afraid at his faithful doubts, and above all not interpret them as "atheism" or "temptation". His doubts are essential components in the maturation process of Christian living.[8]

Temptation

Every Christian life is continually tested to see whether it is built with gold, silver and precious stones, or with wood, hay and stubble (1 Cor. 3. 12). The worst aspect of a Christian life could be that a Christian never notices, or continually forgets, that it is a dangerous undertaking in the most extreme sense. Karl Barth once wrote a new version of the famous passage in Amos (chapter 5), applying it to theologians: "I hate, I despise your lectures and seminars, your sermons, papers and bible commentaries, and I will not smell your discussions, conferences and vacation courses. Though you offer one another and me your hermeneutical, dogmatic, ethical and pastoral recommendations, I will not accept them; neither will I regard the peace offerings of your fat beasts. Take away from me the noise of the old theologians' massive tomes and that of the young theologians' dissertations. And I will not hear the melody of the reviews that you publish in your theological journals, letters and surveys, and in your church and literary papers."[9]

This adaptation also applies (with appropriate variations) to Christian existence as a whole. The most awful thing would be if the Christian were to go gaily on and never once remember or even show that his whole existence is wholly put in question and

[7] Cf. O. A. Rabut, *La vérification religieuse. Recherche d'une Spiritualité pour le Temps de l'Incertitude* (Paris, 1964).

[8] For bibliographical references on the same complex of themes, see L. Boros, "Ich glaube, hilf meinem Unglauben", in *Der gross Entschluss*, 16 (1961), pp. 444–9 and 500–3.

[9] *Ibid.*, pp. 148–9.

endangered by God. The Christ can only have God for himself, if God is also against him all along the line. Perhaps the most trying temptation of Christian existence is to be found on the level of the second and third commandments. When and where is a Christian not guilty of a daring attempt to raise his concepts, images and linguistic constructs to the level of the throne of God, and to worship them. Of course such confusions are subject to that entire incongruity between the living God and what Christians think they ought to say about God. Since God does not tolerate this incongruity, he cannot but be opposed to Christians in their supposed being-Christian. There is a further, quite sublime temptation which seems to befall even the greatest Christians: corruption. It is quite shaking to realize how even the greatest and most respected theologians, such as Athanasius, Augustine, Thomas Aquinas, Luther, Zwingli and Calvin not only left behind positive influences but bequeathed certain malign seeds to us. This is a threat that always hangs over Christian existence in every place. There are no Christians who can live other than out of the merciful loving-kindness of God.[10]

Hope

I am not going at this point to weaken the effect of the foregoing or to take anything away from it. On the contrary, I repeat what I have said, when asserting: The basis of prayerful existence is the "nevertheless" of hope. Christian being is universally directed towards a future that is purely and simply known as "Heaven". Whatever a Christian has to bear in terms of loneliness, doubt and temptation, he will know how to endure in the joy of the Holy Spirit, in an attitude that will eventually emerge triumphantly from its previous shell. In medieval theology "*alacritas*", "*hilaritas*" and "*laetitia spiritualis*" (cheerfulness, happiness and spiritual joy) were essential conditions of the Christian life. Of course a Christian must always remain conscious that his inner joy is the mystery of the grace of God accomplished at Golgotha: the redemption of mankind from disgrace; the new creation of a liberated man, answering the good

[10] The whole question and its ramifications are more exhaustively treated in L. Boros, *In der Versuchung* (Olten, 1968).

faith of God with corresponding loyalty and living in peace with God and to his honour. Thus, but only thus, may the Christian hold up his head in relation to Christ. "Now if we be dead with Christ, we believe that we shall also live with him" (Rom. 6. 8). The decree was enacted in and through Christ, in that he overcame the suffering of loneliness, doubt and temptation. These three have never affected anyone before or after him so radically. And he changed all that into a mercy which is always promise— the revelation of hope.[11]

Silence is Stillness

We are all bound in some way. None of us is absolutely free to move or quite flexible in the hands of God. Therefore we should all say to him: Lord, do not pass by until I have noticed your arrival. Lord, do not stop knocking at my door, beating and pushing against me, until I have opened up to you. Such is the stillness of the man who is ready and willing. The whole essence of that stillness is to be one Yes to God. The most fruitful and inspiring men are always the most peaceful—those who have learned to heed God.

One attains to the innermost depths of Christian existence not when one speaks but when one is silent. When one recollects, inner space opens up and the holy presence of God reveals itself within. One has to learn this stillness. We have to arm ourselves against the endless chatter and boom of this world. Yet external noise is only one half of it all, and perhaps not the half that is most difficult to contend with. The other is inward unrest, the machinery of thought, the round of desire, the anxieties of the heart, and the wall of apathy. Inside us it is like a stream with a pebble-bed. A properly conducted life is versed in the practice of silence. One learns this by really shutting up whenever another's trust, or one's duty, or one's respect for another's life demands it. This should be an obvious apprenticeship for a Christian. But it is only a start. We also have to get used to keep-

[11] On this point I should like to recommend a book that is admittedly not wholly appropriate in its reasoning on every point but is certainly quite justly conceived in its basic ideological argument: J. Moltmann, *Theologie der Hoffnung* (Munich, 1965) (English translation, *Theology of Hope*, London, 1969).

ing silent even when we are expected to speak, to overcoming the longing to talk, a life of chatter. Just think how many super-fluous things we say in the course of a day, and how much that is foolish. We have to learn that silence is golden: that it is not an empty but a genuine and full form of life. And there is more: outward silence is not enough. We have to learn the practice of inward silence: quiet, dwelling on a serious question, an impor-tant task, thinking about someone about whom we are concerned. In so doing we shall experience something worthwhile: that there is an inner human world, a world that grows increasingly pro-found. Ultimately there is stillness before God, before the im-mensity of the one who outbids every faculty and ability to think and feel. All loud and noisy images misfire and break down.

"The Lord is in his holy temple; let all the earth keep silence before him", warns the prophet Habakkuk (Ha. 2. 20). "Keep silence before me ... ; and let the people renew their strength" (Is. 41. 1). "Be silent, O all flesh, before the Lord: for he is raised up out of his holy habitation" (Ze. 2. 17). Thus the prophets predicted the coming of the Redeemer. And when our Lord Christ appeared, it was in the "middle of the night", at a time of great quiet, and to the adoration of shepherds and kings. And the promised eternity is to be filled with an everlasting peace (see Heb. 3. 7–4, 11) which we are not to misinterpret as "inactivity", but understand in all its profundity as "possession of fullness and enjoyment in peace".[12] Much more might be said about quiet as a special "act" of prayer. Here I have been con-cerned only with the basic disposition or inner attitude which first makes any outward prayer possible.

I have tried to describe that basis of Christian existence from which prayer arises. Our Christian prayer is based upon wonder and concern. It entails obligation and loneliness. It has to be sustained in doubt and temptation. Yet hope and rest shine through it. I should like again to stress the fact that the afore-mentioned "conditions for the possibility" of Christian prayer are "present" in any prayer which is made in an appropriately

[12] See L. Boros, *Aus der Hoffnung leben* (Olten, 3rd edn., 1968) and *In der Versuchung* (Olten, 3rd edn., 1968), pp. 97–119.

Christian manner; yet, in outward prayer at one time, one, and at another time another, prerequisite will stand out more and impinge more obviously on the pray-er's conscious mind.

I hope we have really understood the extent to which the underlying structure of our life is permeated by and enclosed in mystery. Not by darkness, but by a light whose brilliance makes our eyes blind and our voice dumb. I should like to quote two sentences from Aquinas, which may serve the reader for peaceful meditation: "The highest stage of all creation is the human soul. Matter strives towards it. . . . Man is the goal of all creation."[13] And: "God is honoured by silence. Not because we wish to say or assert nothing about him, but because we know that we are incapable of conceiving him."[14]

[13] St Thomas Aquinas, *Summa contra Gentes* 3, 22.
[14] Aquinas, *In Trinitate* 2, 1 ad 6.

Translated by John Griffiths

Bernard Besret

Prayer: A Polyphony of Expressions

INTRODUCTION: REQUIREMENTS FOR A LIFE OF PRAYER

SPEAKING of prayer as a "polyphony of expressions" supposes that one has found in one's life, somewhere beyond the aridity in which all prayer seems impossible and derisory, a state of mind in which one rediscovers its meaning, where it can blossom once more. Today, many even of those who have been inspired by the Gospel are still in the middle of an arid desert in this respect, and these reflections on the pluriformity of expressions in prayer may well strike them as wholly fantastic, bearing no relation to their own experience of the Christian life.

It is not my task here to go into the basic possibility of prayer,[1] but it does seem necessary to sketch in, briefly, the contours of the space in which a pluriform prayer can flourish for an individual or a community wishing to live in the breath of the Spirit.

1. *A Living Faith*

This seems to me the first requirement. By a living faith, I do not mean one that has found the answers to all questions and has solved all problems. Neither do I mean a faith with resources of language adequate to express itself with ease and without ambiguity. In any case, we all live our faith in very different ways. But even if faith appears to us as a torment, a chasm opening out

[1] Cf. B. Besret, "Est-il encore possible de prier?", in *Chronique de Boquen*, 5 (March 1972), pp. 5-6.

before us, a probe bored into our flesh, it must be living in us if prayer is to flourish.

Under the pretext of criticism of institutions or of language—both valid and particularly necessary today—we risk leaving life in brackets and so prayer, which is the expression of this life, has nothing further to say and ends by drying up.

2. Freedom of Expression

This is the second requirement. In Western civilization particularly, men are paralysed by all sorts of inhibitions, and their lives are hemmed in by all sorts of restraints, preventing them from expressing themselves and so growing and fulfilling themselves. Frequently victims of anthropological schemata of simplistic dualism, they fail to recognize the body that they are as the place in which to express and fulfil their lives—their spiritual lives included, a fortiori. The first revolution they have to bring about is the liberation of their own bodies to allow them to become the expression and the instrument, or, more briefly and classically, the "efficacious sign", of their whole lives.

3. A Life of Communion

The third and final requirement, within the Christian economy, is to belong to one or more Church communities. One of the essential dimensions of an evangelicad faith is that our relationship with God should be not an individual affair, but should be mediated through our relationships with other men. Our communion with God is indissolubly linked to our communion with men. The various Church cells to which we belong should be at one and the same time a training ground and the shining sign of this double communion.

The first requirement supposes a whole process of learning in faith which is not the direct concern of prayer (even if all prayer, through the effective dimension of the signs it shows, necessarily incorporates a learning process). The second supposes a whole art of living, a wisdom of man and his body which, besides affecting his everyday, immediate life, also involves political requirements for the organization of men's lives in community. This ascesis for our time is not the immediate concern of prayer either (though here too all prayer, through the effective dimensions of the signs it shows, involves men in living a certain ascesis). Finally, the third requirement supposes a living tissue of Church cells in communion with each other in the same spirit, the same hope, the same love. This ecclesial task, in its turn, goes far beyond what prayer can bring about, though it remains true that community prayer, through the effective dimension of the signs it shows, is one of the high points, perhaps the highest, of life in communion.

Prayer in itself, however, cannot be a substitute either for instruction, through which faith should be constantly enlivened and deepened in the life of an individual or a community, or for the ascesis through which they should rid themselves of all internal and external aberrations, or for the life of the Church which should be a source of refreshment to the faithful in the world. All these elements are necessary to the development of a life regenerated by the Spirit: prayer is but the outcome of this life on the level of expression. On this level, there are no "recipes" for an authentic prayer independent of the life this prayer expresses and, through a process of feedback, develops. When signs start to take the place of life, we are drifting into hypocrisy and pharisaism. But, on the other hand, there can be no development in the life of an individual or a community without expression through all the registers at man's command—and this is the point at which prayer springs forth.

It would be presumptuous to try to list every note going to make up the vast repertoire of expression covered by prayer. I prefer to discuss three themes, which correspond to three types of experience.

I. Prayer of the Body

1. *Realizing that One is a Body*

Prayer has no need of words. Words that are not a response to a real inner need are often in danger of being no more than a screen against a true confrontation with life and the Spirit, a less painful way of passing the time. So many prayers founder in the sands of verbalizing that is no more than verbiage. A pretence at prayer.

In order to pray, the first requirement is that one be there, present, an awakened consciousness here and now in the body that I am and feel. Pausing to take stock of this existence in the world that we are, here incarnate, is a first and very basic form of prayer. I have to take myself, such as I am, before I can give myself. But this simple taking stock, this recollection in the face of the agitation and dispersion of my activity, leads me to an imperceptible change of posture. My body comes into play: my legs stretch; my back straightens. My clavicles ("keys" to our posture, as their name indicates) seek the horizontal. Instinctively, we begin to lose some of the tensions we build up to play our role in society; the channels of breathing and the arteries relax and unblock, as do those of that mysterious life force that Western medicine hardly recognizes, but which lies at the heart of Eastern wisdom and medicine.

One can of course carry out this instinctive redressing of posture as a conscious act, thereby establishing a real interplay between one's consciousness of being there and one's manner of being there: a mutual causality. Every improvement of one brings about a modification of the other.

So here I am, now, present. Wordless, this is my first act of thanksgiving: taking note of God's gift of life. Without this attention to the life we possess, if we are constantly losing sight of it, we cannot give thanks. And it is no use thinking we can be attentive in this way without our bodies living this attention, being transformed by it, and in turn transforming it. Hence the accumulated wisdom of postures for prayer, which are by no means folklore or superstition. There is a certain efficacy inherent in these postures—which also means that they can be objectively assessed and stripped of the absolute character they tend to assume when they become a "rite" and take on a directly sacral value they do not *ipso facto* possess.

2. *Breathing*

Finding a posture favourable to a lively appreciation of the life in us can be a prayer in itself. A gift received and promptly offered back, an acceptance of the great rhythm of creation and a thanksgiving that is also self-abandonment. And then within this process of acceptance and offering, I feel my breathing carrying me along at its rhythm, which, made up of breathing in and breathing out, is also one of acceptance and abandonment. My breathing becomes a prayer; my prayer becomes breathing. It is no mere chance that the Hebrew words for breath, life, soul, spirit and wind all have the same root. Breathing out, I give myself, abandon myself, increase my capacity for receiving yet more life. Then, breathing in, I find myself again; with the air I breathe I give a welcome to life, to the spirit, the gift of God.[2]

3. Voiced Breathing

My prayer can continue and develop as a silence phased by my breathing in, out, and in again. But it can also acquire a voice. My breathing out, starting from deep down inside me, becomes a shudder that shakes me inside and then changes into vibrating sounds that, in their turn, have a subtle effect on the whole surface of my body,[3] accentuating still further my consciousness of existing here and now, present and yet abandoned to this vibration which expresses me and extends me beyond myself.

I could pursue this line of development further, to show how vibration can become modulation, modulation become word and song, the community that prays become a community of love. But then I would have to restrict this article too much to one type of experience only, and so over-emphasize one approach that has nothing particularly evangelical about it, and indeed, nothing particularly logical in its approach outside the stages I have pointed out. There are of course other possible approaches, other developments, other dynamisms, not necessarily contradictory to the first approach.

II. Prayer of the Heart

1. Ruminating on the Word

Our first approach to prayer was made up of silence or nonverbal sounds, as a reaction against excessive verbalizing in prayer. But the Gospel is the word, the announcement of the good news, and the life of an individual or a community that looks to the good news for participation in the spirit of Christ

[2] Cf. K. von Dürckheim, *Der Alltag als Übung* (Berne, 1966).
[3] Cf. A. Tomatis, *L'oreille et le langage* (Paris, 1963), p. 73.

consists in assimilating this word, giving it life, allowing it to become flesh and dwell amongst men.

This can be the starting-point for another process of prayer. Not a matter of piling up words into a conceptual discourse—this belongs to another movement of the Christian life—but rather one of intuitively grasping the mystery that all these words are trying to express, of becoming one with it, of seizing the deep unity between the life that animates us and the life that shines through the history to which Scripture gives witness. One word can be enough, or a single sentence, perhaps. The ancients spoke of "ruminating". They ruminated the Psalms and verses of the gospels. The word then became their bread. "Man does not live by bread alone, but by every word that comes from the mouth of God" (Matt. 4. 4). Men have lived on the name of Jesus alone, the name that means "God saves".

2. Sighs of Gratitude too deep for Words

At times even this word will be unnecessary, and the mystery perceived will appear inexpressible. Man will not be able to find words for it, and his only means of expressing it will be by "sighs too deep for words" (Rom. 8. 26), a sharing of St Paul's experience, as described in the Epistle to the Galatians: "And the proof that you are sons is that God has sent into our hearts the Spirit of his Son, which cries: Abba, Father" (Gal. 4. 6).

It is no use waiting for this cry to issue forth of its own accord, as if the Spirit could force it on us from outside. It can only come as the result of a long process of assimilation of the good news of the Gospel, and of meditation on the "mystery" that should transform our relations with God and man. It is only a constantly alert faith that can look at the world through Jesus' eyes, come to cry: "Abba, Father", and base all its prayer on this cry, a cry that comes not from the shock of a particular event, but from the steady pressure of a well-nourished faith.

3. Sighs of Sorrow and a Cry for Help

Man's experience is not limited to the life he receives and the life he gives, to the love of God seen in the love of men. He also experiences setbacks, periods of being unable to act, suffering and death. Prayer can then become the sighs of the oppressed reaching out for liberation. Here it will be sorrow that deprives him of words or phrases, and the Spirit will help his weakness and intercede for him with "sighs too deep for words" when he cries for help as one who can do no more, who has reached the end of his tether.

In this state, he will not care much for vocabulary or grammar; still less for finely turned phrases. He cries out and puts the whole of his being into this cry. It cannot be categorized or programmed without becoming artificial, and by the same token it cannot be incorporated into a liturgy without seeming ridiculous or affected. If it does not come from the stress of life itself, it cannot be authentic.

III. COMMUNAL PRAYER

Having considered prayer attuned to the rhythm of our lives, and prayer nourished by long meditation on the Gospel and the events of our lives, we must now turn to communal prayer. This occupies an important place in Christian experience to the extent that this links communion with God ineluctably to communion among men. When they assemble to pray together, Christians are seeking to show forth the mystery they live, to make it consciously present. This mystery is at once communion among brothers, communion in the same spirit, and, in the last analysis, communion with God.

1. The Link with Life

Each community has a history. The final movement of prayer does not start from nothing; it is part of a sequence of life. If it changes key, it is only the key of its expression; not living something different, but living the same thing in a different way, on a different level of consciousness and expression. Neither communal prayer nor the celebration of the Eucharist will miraculously make love blossom on stony or hostile ground. Here too there has to be give and take, a mutual causality, between life and its expression.

2. The Place

Men and women assembled: part of a vast throng. The place

where they assemble has a certain importance: some places bring people together; others tend to push them apart. Some force a style of behaviour on you (by their design and furnishings); others free you and put you at your ease. It is not a question of the money that has been spent on a place, but of its spirit. So many of our churches, with their static plan, and their pews in straight lines, kill all hope and creativity, so that it would need exceptional vitality to extract a meaningful form of prayer from such a rigid mould.

3. Clothes

The same applies to clothes: some force you to play a role; others can help to hide superficial and alienating definitions of personality. If one can criticize liturgical dress, it is on the grounds that it has become the exclusive property of a sacralized caste, and, in turn, forces those who wear it to play an artificial part in the assembly. But perhaps there will come a day when the whole Christian community will decide to constitute itself and show itself as a Christian community, putting off the old man on the threshold of the assembly to put on the armour of light: "All of you, baptized in Christ, have put on Christ; there is no more Jew nor Greek, no more slave nor free man, because you are all one in Christ Jesus" (Gal. 3. 27–28). Clothing can then become a call to conversion, a hope of salvation: it can become prayer.

4. A Welcome to Others

The transition from "private prayer" to communal prayer should not involve any break. The quest for self-knowledge and for presence to oneself, far from being rendered useless, becomes even more necessary as it changes into a capacity for welcoming others, for receiving and giving. If we are to communicate with others, we must all be present.

There are many ways of welcoming others, and the most obvious are not necessarily the most effective. The quality of a gesture can often be measured by its discretion, not to be confused with a fearful reserve that is rather the mark of an attitude of hostility, of a refusal to receive and to give. Bodily contact is a first sign of communion and often an effective way of measuring the distances that separate us and the work we still have to do if we are to teach ourselves really to love.

5. *Silence and Awakening*

For a word to resound in the assembly, call it together, provoke it to an awakening of its evangelical consciousness, make it feel the urgency of converting the old world in which we all habitually live to a new world in which the Spirit of Jesus can rule over the earth—for a word to do all this, it must dig the furrow of attention needed to give it a fertile soil. A word spoken amidst general inattention is a word lost (except, perhaps, to the speaker). But silence in itself is not enough to capture attention: silence can be a fullness, but it can also be sheer absence of sound, as empty of communication and mystery as the silence in a dentist's waiting-room. To be a fullness, it has to consist of the active presence of each to everyone else, and of all to that mysterious reality we call God.

A background of sound, provided it does not become the object of attention in itself, forcing the members of the assembly into the fragmented role of a passive audience in a concert hall, can be an effective way of creating an awakened state of mind and of attracting everyone's attention together.

Singing can also have this effect. But if the members of the community are accustomed to finding their own level of vibration and can emit it in tranquillity, then the collective improvisation built up from all these murmers is perhaps to every- of the most effective ways of making everyone present to everyone else. This is, however, by no means a universal panacea, since experience shows that it can only work if each member of the group is adequately reconciled to himself and to all the other members; otherwise one's murmur sticks in the back of one's throat and refuses to emerge. Where there is any tension or lack of communion, playing music or singing will help, but there can be no true vibration in tune with others.

6. *The Word goes forth*

In such a silence charged with attention and so with expectation, a word can really resound. It can be read, proclaimed, muttered or shouted. It can come from a book or it can be re-created by the assembly, a collective poem in which each will bring his word to the building-up of the Word. Knowing how to make up the Word is as much part of being a Christian as knowing how to receive it from the pulpit. If the spirit that inspires an assembly is the same Spirit that inspired the prophets and the evangelists, it will breathe the same Word to it even if it is expressed in other words.

Liturgy then becomes a "happening", a unique event, here and now, for *this* community, at *this* precise moment in its history. Not that the assembly will then, like Narcissus, contemplate itself in the mirror it holds up to itself at this unique moment: one or other of its members will take on the task of reminding it of God's plan, of the demands of his love and the practical and political implications of his Gospel. The assembly can trust in the Spirit.

Then the whole assembly will be the celebrant.

Translated by Paul Burns

Josef Bommer

Is the Prayer of Petition and Intercession still Meaningful?

I. THE CRISIS

PERSONAL prayer is undoubtedly going through a period of crisis and the gravest crisis of all is being experienced in the sphere of the prayer of petition, which is, after all, the form of prayer most stressed in Jesus' teaching. A striking example of this crisis can be found in Bertold Brecht's play, *Mother Courage and her Children*. A group of terrified peasants are waiting for the soldiers to attack the neighbouring town by night, in the growing conviction that they can do nothing to prevent it. Their conclusion is—if you can do nothing, you can at least pray. While they are praying, the dumb girl Kattrin gets up, fetches a drum, climbs onto a farmyard roof and saves the town by the noise of her drumming.[1]

The prayer of petition is criticized by scientists, who regard it as a purely illusion faith in God's providence which contradicts the laws of natural science. The psychological objection is that prayer is based on an egocentric assumption that God's control of the world is dependent on the desires of the person praying, who can, in this way, gain power over God. Prayer originally meant "exercising power",[2] was closely related to the practice of magic and laid claims to God himself. A third criticism is that

[1] D. Sölle, *Atheistisch an Gott glauben* (Olten ²1969), p. 111; G. G. Otto, *Über das Gebet*. Gebet und Gebetserziehung, Pädagogische Forschungen, Veröffentlichungen des Comenius-Instituts (Heidelberg, 1971), p. 42.
[2] G. van der Leeuw, *Phänomenologie der Religion* (Tübingen, 1946), pp. 480 ff.

prayer enables the Christian to forget his responsibilities to society.

Two fundamental theological problems underlie these three criticisms—contemporary man's concept of God and his attitude towards the world. In the first case, the crisis affecting the traditional concept of a personal God has led many believers to wonder whether the practice of petition can still be taken seriously by modern man. The theological attack against God's personality is having repercussions on the personal character of prayer, which, as petition, still has the traditional form of an I-thou relationship. In the second case, man's changed understanding of the world has led him to reject the idea of God as a moral, political and scientific stopgap. All the assumptions that have, in the past, been made about petitionary prayer are undermined as soon as man is no longer at the mercy of nature as blind fate and the world as a phenomenon where effect follows cause without reference to his responsible control. Who, for instance, really believes nowadays that God will put an end to the war in Vietnam, hunger in Pakistan or the incurable cancer from which his wife is suffering, however earnestly we pray for this in our private or public intercessions?

In considering the whole question of petitionary or intercessory prayer, we have above all to bear in mind the purely limited help that can be provided by biblical pronouncements, which were originally made by men whose thought and attitude towards the world were very different from our own. Hermeneutics can hardly be avoided here and a critical examination of the nature and function of petitionary prayer and, for example, of the bidding prayers in the celebration of the Eucharist is certainly necessary if these are to be more than pure routine. I should like to do this under three headings, corresponding with the three types of answer given by contemporary German writers on the subject of prayer.

II. SUGGESTED SOLUTIONS

1. *The Traditional Theological Solution*

This solution is based on two assumptions, firstly that God and man have a personal relationship with each other and

secondly that this relationship is direct. Both Catholic and Pro-
testant spirituality is still to a great extent conditioned by this
traditional attitude towards prayer as talking with a God who
has revealed himself directly in the person of Jesus, thus, as
Brunner has said, "making it possible for man, isolated, without
love and prayer, in himself" to call upon him in the name of
Jesus.[3] We can make our requests known to God in an atmosphere of direct personal trust and intimacy—man is a child
talking to God his father, and why should our heavenly Father
not grant our requests if our father on earth does so (see Luke
11. 9-13)? The simple confidence of "ask, and it will be given
you; seek, and you will find; knock, and it will be opened to
you" (Matt. 7. 7) and of "your heavenly Father knows that you
need all these things" (Matt. 6. 32) is to be found in this attitude, which is one of conformity to the will of God, praying "in
the name of Jesus" and always modifying our own desires by
asking only if what we want is in accordance with God's will.
In this way, we can be sure that it is the Spirit of Christ praying
in us, because we do not ourselves "know how to pray as we
ought" (Rom. 8. 26).

This traditional type of prayer begins with a very real request
for bread, then rises to an absolute trust in God and ends with
unconditional surrender to his will. It takes place within the
framework of God's revelation of himself in Jesus Christ and the
Church and, although its content may alter, the situation in
which prayer takes place remains the same and is determined by
God. God literally places himself completely at everyone's dis-
posal, certainly according to the parable of the importunate
friend (Luke 11. 5-8). The great exponent of the prayer of intercession is, of course, Paul, who recognized that it stemmed from
the community of believers and led to an increase in solidarity
and mutual responsibility (Col. 1. 24; 1 Cor. 12. 12).

Intercession has been described as "an offer that we should not
refuse because there is a great need in the world and we are
responsible for that need as Christians, but are not equal to that
responsibility".[4] The Christian acknowledges this need in his

[3] E. Brunner, *Dogmatik III. Die christliche Lehre von der Kirche, vom
Glauben und von der Vollendung* (Zürich, [2]1964), p. 369.
[4] S. Hausamann, "Atheistisch zu Gott beten?", *Evangelische Theologie*,
8 (1971), p. 414.

intercession and hopes that God will touch men's hearts, guide their thoughts, strengthen their sense of responsibility and give them courage to act. Yet—and this is important—in confidently expecting real help from the personal God whom he addresses as "thou" in prayer, man will, in accordance with his contemporary view of the world, not pray that his house will not be destroyed by lightning, but will erect a lightning conductor on the roof and will not pray for rain, but will instal watering devices in his fields. He will, in other words, take the initiative himself rather than count on God's help. His own attitude to prayer has to change and he has to recognize that God will not do what we can and should do and that God will not break through the natural laws of the world.

We may conclude by saying that this ontological interpretation of a personally anthropomorphic and biblical way of speaking results in a perfectionist view of prayer in which there is no room for doubt. The child prays to the father and experiences the closeness of God. I speak and God hears.

2. *The Anthropological Solution*

What is above all called into question in this second proposed solution to the problem is the personal nature of God. The criticism that is made of this solution is that, in it, the relationship between God and man, as described in the Bible, is raised to the level of an ontological statement about God's personality and qualified as a purely Christian statement.

According to Heinrich Ott, for example, "whenever we speak of a personal God, we do not assign to him a category that we can ourselves grasp, but rather relate our standing before him to our lack of experience of his personal character. Whenever we say 'God', this can only imply that we associate as closely with him as with our fellow men and as historically, although this association is at the same time quite different from the one we enjoy with our fellow men, hence the doctrine of the trinity".[5] The hermeneutical question as to whether a basic anthropological category may not perhaps be necessary for our interpretation of the reality of God is thus explicitly refuted as illegitimate.

Walter Bernet has taken up the most extreme position of theo-

[5] H. Ott, *Wirklichkeit und Glaube*, 1 (Zürich, 1966), p. 317.

logical a-personalism in the question of prayer. In his book *Gebet*,[6] he says, for instance, "It is, in my opinion, perfectly logical to insist that all 'speaking about God' is, according to my view of prayer, a 'question about God', something that is remote from the customary theological categories, both personal and soteriological. This does not in any way imply a restricted linguistic diet—I have no objection, for instance, to addressing God in prayer using the intimate word 'thou'—but I am convinced that theologians are bound, because of man's experience, to go beyond the categories of personality and soteriology if they are to be able to give a place to the question about God."[7]

For Bernet, prayer is closely related to experience and an important part is also played by the Absolute, which appears in prayer as a mysterious question. Bernet defines prayer as an act of thinking in which experience reflects and reflected experience is narrated.[8] He concludes that prayer, including that of petition and intercession, has the three basic functions of reflecting, narrating and situating.

Prayer therefore does not enable us to reach a personal God, because this God can no longer be thought of as objectively confronting us. Prayer is not a dialogue with God—it is rather a basic human activity, in which man expresses, commits and involves himself. As Dorothee Sölle says, "Praying oneself is expressing oneself. . . . In the Our Father, we ourselves are expressed, we whose Father is a long way away, in heaven, we who need the name, the kingdom and the will of God, but who do not have them with us, we the hungry, the guilty and the tempted. We ourselves are the content of our prayer. The Our Father tries to say *us*. . . . In prayer, the real man is expressed. . . . Our experience of the world, which fashions us, is expressed."[9] Accord-

[6] W. Bernet, *Gebet* (Themen der Theologie, 6) (Stuttgart, 1970).
[7] W. Bernet, *op. cit.*, p. 166.
[8] W. Bernet, *op. cit.*, p. 165.
[9] D. Sölle, *Die Wahrheit ist konkret* (Olten, [5]1969), pp. 109–11. Three statements in the same authoress' *Politisches Nachtgebet in Köln* (Stuttgart and Mainz, [3]1969), pp. 24–5, are relevant in this context. They are thesis 2: "Prayer prepares man to accept responsibility for his world. God's activity is therefore not put forward as a substitute for man's activity"; thesis 6: "In the petition that he formulates in his prayer, man expresses himself before God in his anguish because God's kingdom has still not

ing to this view of prayer, then, man himself is wholly involved and expressed. In the prayer of petition, there is no place for any desire to have an influence, perhaps even a magic effect, on God. Man expresses himself rather as the one who is in need, who has not given up hope and whose prayer is therefore a profoundly human process. It is precisely for this reason that the prayer of petition played such an important part in the life of Jesus. In a human situation of need, impotence, poverty and hope, it is not praise and thanksgiving, but petition which is the only really appropriate prayer, because man has to express himself as man, in all his neediness, and God does not, in this situation, confront him as a *Deus ex machina* who can be addressed directly.

The prayer of intercession, however, should never be a substitute for action. It should above all be a raising up of the situation to God. Those making the intercession reflect about the situation and create a visible solidarity within the community of believers. Intercession can only indirectly be of help to those for whom prayer is offered, by making those who offer it themselves more human and more open to any kind of help. In this way, intercessory prayer can help to make the world a better place. The person praying has to pray for the part of the world for which he feels co-responsible. In this way, he will avoid using prayer as an excuse for failing to act.

This, of course, is the basis for the "non-religious" prayer of petition and intercession that is directed towards one's fellow men.[10] As J. A. T. Robinson has pointed out, "to open oneself to another *unconditionally* in love *is* to be with him in the presence of God, and that is the heart of intercession. To pray for another is to expose both oneself and him to the common ground of our being. . . . It may not be talking *to* God . . . , about him at all. The *Thou* addressed may be his own *Thou*, but it may be addressed and responded to at such a level that we can

---

come, in his hope that it will come and in his responsibility for helping to bring it about. In his prayer of petition, man makes God's cause his own"; and finally, her thesis 7: "Even in those situations where man can no longer be helped by his fellow men and where he is no longer able to act, the prayer of petition keeps his longing for the kingdom of God alive, makes him more human and prevents him from despairing in the ultimate meaning of the world."

[10] J. A. T. Robinson, *Honest to God* (London, 1963), pp. 99 ff.

only speak of knowing him in God and God in him. . . . Prayer is the responsibility to meet others with *all* I have."[11] In this sense, prayer within the context of an I-Thou relationship with our fellow men can be exactly the same as love of our fellow men.

Herbert Braun's point of departure is somewhat different. He is above all concerned with meditation, which, he claims, enables the believer to feel assured that he is sustained by what he calls the "origin of what I am obliged and of what I am permitted to do". What is the object of prayer? he asks and replies: "I do not pray to preserve my reputation as a devout Christian . . . with others in mind. Do I pray, then, because of God? . . . No, I do not pray for the sake of God. For whose sake do I pray, then? God does not have to be informed by my prayers. Nor does he have to be stimulated to action by my prayers. I am the one who is to be helped by my prayers."[12]

Gert Otto has tried to compare and contrast these ideas about prayer, which are not based on an unbroken personal relationship between God and man, with prayer in the New Testament,[13] in which prayer is presented in various ways. Although it was automatically accepted in later antiquity, it is not accepted today firstly that God can and does intervene directly in the course of the world and secondly that man can invoke God, who in turn offers help as a mediator. "Is it possible for us to go beyond pure historical knowledge and really make our own the understanding of God and the world that is contained in these two New Testament ideas, reproducing them in our contemporary practice of prayer? I think not."[14]

Otto has, however, pointed to another series of statements in the New Testament, especially in the writings of Paul, which are strikingly distinct from the view concerning prayer and religiosity that prevailed generally in the ancient world and are basically "non-religious" in tone. They can be summarized under the title of "pray constantly" (1 Thess. 5. 17), which removes prayer from its purely cultic context, lifts it out of the sphere of individual and isolated action performed at certain times and

[11] J. A. T. Robinson, *op. cit.*, pp. 99–100.
[12] H. Braun, *Göttinger Preditmeditationen* (Berlin, 1964–1965), p. 168.
[13] G. Otto, *op. cit.*, pp. 31–8.
[14] G. Otto, *op. cit.*, p. 34.

according to certain formulae and places it within the much wider context of an attitude to life. As Otto has pointed out, the New Testament contains not only prayers addressing God as "thou", but also prayers referring to God as "he", thus blurring the distinction between prayer to God and reflection about God. An example of this is Rom. 11. 34 ff.: "For who has known the mind of the Lord, or who has been his counsellor?... For from him and through him and to him are all things. To him be honour and glory for ever. Amen." This "prayer" is basically leaving in God's hands the mystery as it presents itself to man on reflection.

Prayer, then, implies not an individual or isolated pious action, but first and foremost an attitude embracing the whole of life. "Prayer", Otto says, "is not the point of departure for pious practices, nor does it provide proof of piety. It is rather the place where man reflects about the manner and form of his life and his conscience."[15]

We may conclude this summary of the views of those who favour an anthropological solution to the problem of prayer today by saying that this solution offers many possibilities, but the consequences are not always very easy to draw. What all these possible solutions have in common, however, is that they all favour the idea of prayer, not as a relationship between man and a personal God, but as an attempt on man's part to understand himself and God and to reflect about his life.

3. Prayer in Secondary Immediacy[16]

According to a third group of theologians, the experience of modern man and the situation within which he is trying to pray are not sufficiently reflected either in the naïve I-thou relationship of the first solution outlined above or in the second point of view, which neglects certain "vertical" aspects of prayer in favour of the purely horizontal relationship. They have therefore attempted to find a position in the problem of prayer midway

[15] G. Otto, op. cit., p. 40.
[16] A term used by H. Schultze in his article on doubt and trust in prayer, "Gebet zwischen Zweifel und Vertrauen", in Evangelische Theologie, 3 (1970), pp. 133-49.

between the first, traditional point of view and the second, anthropological solution.

H. Schultze, who is representative of this group, says that prayer is always challenged and exposed to doubt. "Our prayer is part of our activity in faith in the provisional state of our journey through life as pilgrims."[17] This is why "we do not know how to pray as we ought" (Rom. 8. 26). Faith is challenged and questioned because man himself lives in a situation that is seldom translucent. "All prayer", Schultze has said, "is provisional and takes place at the level of a question that can only be resolved at the discretion of the individual himself (Mark 14. 36). It is therefore dependent on the Spirit acting as representative and on the glorified Christ interceding for us."[18] Paul discusses this questionable and uncertain character of prayer in 2 Cor. 12. 7–9. Our weakness and our constant exposure to doubt and challenge determines the situation within which we pray. We always pray as sinners. Faith and lack of faith exist side by side in us, so that prayer can never simply express faith alone (Mark 9. 24)—it also expresses the whole challenged personality of the person praying.

In addition to being challenged, Christians are also exposed to doubt. Whether they still pray or whether they have long since given up the practice of prayer, they will still say, "We prayed and God did not answer. We called out and God remained silent. . . We could have proved to him how modest and easily satisfied our demands were. . . ." They will go on to enumerate the occasions when God in fact remained silent—when we prayed for starving children, for raped girls, for young people beaten to death, for exploited workers, for deceived women, for the victims of injustice. . . .[19]

Modern man can only be helped by regarding this doubt as an integral part of the situation within which he tries to pray. He can, after all, readily acknowledge his debt to Jeremiah and Job in the art of prayer—their faith too was challenged and questioned, they both believed and disbelieved, accused God and rebelled against him in prayer.

[17] H. Schultze, *op. cit.*, p. 141.
[18] H. Schultze, *op. cit.*, p. 142.
[19] K. Rahner, *Von der Not und vom Segen des Gebetes* (Freiburg, ³1960), p. 77.

In letting God help us to overcome our doubt and the situation of challenge, not once but again and again, we are given a new secondary immediacy.[20] This psychological term is appropriate in this context because trust and self-surrender do not take place at the level of naïve primary immediacy, but have to pass through mature reflection to the stage of secondary immediacy.[21] There is, then, a process of growth in prayer—from the prayer of the child, through doubt and a situation of challenge, faith and lack of faith, to that of the mature son. The new form of prayer that we are given when we reach this stage of secondary immediacy through reflection can perhaps best be described in the form of personal prayer.

We may conclude by quoting Schultze again. "Meditation and action (Braun and Robinson) are both very restricted in their possibilities. They represent opposite poles and as such the impossibility of replacing personal prayer with an adequate equivalent. It would in fact seem that there is no better response in faith to God's saving activity than personal prayer of the traditional kind. Faith can no longer be related in this new situation to an ontological relationship with a personal God. The problem of knowledge persists. All the same, man has still, in faith, to address God, to thank him, to complain to him and to make demands on him. This is not a mere analogy any more than real commitment and love are analogies. On the contrary—in prayer, we are, if the Holy Spirit makes his abode in us, able even now to experience something of the fellowship of God of the new era."[22]

[20] H. Schultze, op. cit., p. 147.
[21] P. Lersch, Der Aufbau der Person (Munich, 1954).
[22] H. Schultze, op. cit., p. 149.

Translated by David Smith

PART II
BULLETIN

Josephine Massingberd Ford

Pentecostal Catholicism

Definition

CATHOLIC Neo-Pentecostalism[1] is a prayer movement within the
Roman Catholic Church, which is characterized by use of the
preternatural gifts such as tongues, healing, prophecy, etc. Its
members frequently undergo an initial conversion experience
which either draws them from a life of sin or unbelief or, if
they are already practising Christians, to a deeper commitment
(probably this would be called "second conversion" in traditional
spirituality). The experience appears to be accompanied by a
touch (*not* the state) of infused contemplation which may last a
few minutes or even a few days: for many this is followed by a
sensible devotion akin to "converts' fervour". This conversion
experience is termed "baptism of the Spirit" by the Pentecostals
but the more accurate term would be "release of the Spirit".
Not infrequently the gift of tongues, that is, the facility to speak
a language unlearnt in the human way, accompanies this conversion. Without any doubt the experience has a psychological
aspect. In some cases "tongues" appear to be psychologically in-

[1] Further details are given in the author's paper "Catholic Neo-Pentecostalism, the Radical Reformation and Sensitivity Groups" submitted to
Theological Studies. Pertinent books are: K. D. Ranaghan, *Catholic Pentecostals* (Paulist Press, 1969); J. Massingberd Ford, *The Pentecostal Experience* (Paulist Press, 1970); E. D. O'Connor, *The Pentecostal Movement
in the Catholic Church* (Ave Maria Press, 1971); D. Gelpi, *Catholic Pentecostalism* (Paulist Press, 1971); J. Massingberd Ford, *Baptism of the Spirit*
(Claretian Press, 1971); Kilian McDonnell, *Catholic Pentecostalism, Problems in Evaluation* (Dove Publication, Pecos, New Mexico).

duced. However, Pentecostals appear to be as normal psychologically as other people. Indeed, the Pentecostal experience does appear to give a temporary relief to psychological problems and has not infrequently united partners in marriage and amended other human relationships: however, it would appear advisable for persons thus affected to continue to receive professional help, for the Holy Spirit may begin a healing but expect our human co-operation to continue it.

Pentecostals show a lively interest in prayer, especially spontaneous prayer, a thirst for Scripture, usually an increasing devotion to the sacraments, sometimes a love for Mary, a faith in supernatural intervention, a peace, joy and love especially for their fellow Pentecostals: many seem to enjoy a sense of the presence of God. Although some show social concern this does not appear to be characteristic of the movement itself.

Pentecostal prayer meetings are similar to that which is described in 1 Cor. 14. 26–33. They comprise hymn singing, testimony prophecy (not prediction but usually a prophetic or biblically phrased utterance inspired by the Holy Spirit but also fused with a person's human qualities); Scripture reading and reflection, spontaneous prayer, silence, speaking in tongues with interpretation and sometimes a prepared talk. They are followed by a session for personal ministry, i.e., imposition of hands and prayer for various intentions. The meetings spread an atmosphere of joy, love, peace and lively faith. Guitars or other musical instruments are used and there is sometimes clapping of hands but Catholic Pentecostal meetings tend to be much quieter and less exuberant than mainline Pentecostal ones.

The Pentecostal spirituality has exhibited most of the ministries of the Spirit which are listed in 1 Cor. 12. 4–11 but it would seem that it has still to develop these gifts into a wider dimension than that of the purely preternatural. For example, cultic prophecy should mature into prophetic action on an ecclesial, social and political level; and the utterance of wisdom needs to be combined with intellectual competence

History

Pentecostalism had its first "public" manifestation in association with Duquesne University in Pittsburgh, Pennsylvania, in

1967 when professors and students on retreat received the experience described above. Three of the leading figures have passed beyond that experience into extremely productive work in Church renewal and in their professional spheres, but formally they do not belong to the movement. From Duquesne the movement spread to Notre Dame, South Bend, Indiana, and subsequently over America and Canada, and small groups developed in the West Indies, Latin America, England, Ireland, Spain, Lebanon, Australia, Philippines, Korea, Taiwan, New Zealand and Thailand. In August 1971 the Directory of the Catholic Charismatic Prayer Groups listed about 305 prayer groups. For the last five years there has been an international conference held at Notre Dame/St Mary's, Indiana, in June: last year 4,500 attended and 10,000 are expected this year. A leaders' meeting is held each January at Ann Arbor, Michigan, but this is now being divided into regional meetings. The organization and large majority of talks at each conference are in the hands of the leaders at Ann Arbor and Notre Dame/South Bend although a more representative advisory committee was formed last year. Pentecostalism draws people of all ages and social positions but has occurred especially in University circles. It is akin to, but not identified with, the Jesus Freak movement. The U.S. bishops countenanced the movement in 1969 but have not pronounced finally upon it.

Theology

A critical theology of the movement has yet to be developed and some confusion has been caused by the fact that exponents of Pentecostal spirituality are inclined to borrow terms and sometimes practices from mainline Pentecostals. As far as the present writer can discern there are two trends developing within American Catholic Pentecostalism. One trend emanates from the most influential centres, Ann Arbor in Michigan and Notre Dame and their friends, and may be seen as a structured Pentecostalism; the other trend is a free Pentecostalism which is more integrated with other movements of the Holy Spirit. A study of books, pamphlets, unpublished material and tape recordings of talks given at the conferences reveals the fact that the community aspect of Pentecostalism has taken a definite shape during the last eighteen months. Entry into the covenant community is procured as follows. There is a catechumenate of six weeks' duration which culminates in imposition of hands and prayer for the "baptism of the Spirit". The gift of tongues is given special prominence. After this initiation the candidate attends further seminars and gains admission into the covenant groups through a public declaration of his or her willingness to accept the covenant and the discipline of the community. Membership is limited to those baptized in the Spirit in the Pentecostal way but open to non-Roman Catholics: approximately one-third of the Ann Arbor community is non-Catholic. That these communities are more than religious congregations is suggested by the emergence of a complete para-ecclesial structure. Offices are modelled on those found in the Pastoral epistles but the titles differ: overall co-ordinator = bishop; co-ordinator = elder or presbyter and servant = deacon and handmaid = deaconess. At Ann Arbor, the co-ordinators are installed with a ceremony at a community meeting. They are regarded "as a body through whom the Lord can speak"; they require almost absolute obedience from their subordinates and claim the authority to exclude members from the community and to impose shunning on the basis of Matt. 18 and 1 Cor. 5 respectively. At Ann Arbor and Notre Dame/South Bend the same laymen have been in office from the beginning but at San Francisco the offices are for one year and a priest is one of the overall co-ordinators. Thus, the present writer, while not doubting the sincerity and commitment of the persons concerned or the success of their mission with regard to numbers joining their community or converted to a better life would question the adequacy of their theology. One trusts that these leaders will have the wisdom to seek professional help through theologians, psychologists and sociologists to increase the blessings emanating from their Christian community: they are surely aware that genuine faith and religious experience can sustain scholarly investigation.

On the other hand many of the other prayer groups throughout the country appear to be un-influenced by the Ann Arbor–Notre Dame spirituality. The present writer sent a questionnaire to all the prayer groups listed in the Directory: 290 questionnaires appear to have reached their destination and 130 completed forms were returned. The findings are most encouraging. Although approximately 90 groups use the Ann Arbor catechumenate, very few groups appear to have adopted the para-ecclesial structure. Only 10 have covenant agreements; only 19 have formal officers and only 27 agree to the use of the exclusion texts cited above: many were sharply opposed to such a practice. The groups show quite a breadth of variety. In the "secular" (in distinction from the religious) groups the number of members ranges from 3 to 500; 90 had under 100; 15 had between 100 and 200; 5 between 200–300 and 3 between 300–500. The percentage of Roman Catholics was interesting: 64 groups had over 90%; 29 groups between 70–90%; 16 between 40–65% and 3 below 40%. The lowest was 5%. The groups are predominantly white, 53 being all white; 43 having over 90% white; 3 over 60% white and 3 over 50%. One group comprised 70% Indians and one group 80% Chicanoes. The time devoted to the prayer meeting lasted from one and one-half to five or six hours and comprised teaching, prayer and "body ministry". Sixty-two groups combined liturgical functions with the prayer meeting. Although the books which the group read were almost wholly Pentecostal, people's interests did not seem to be restricted to Pentecostalism but many took an active part in the non-Pentecostal parish activities and, as individuals, engaged in social action. From the questionnaires the writer could detect no anti-intellectualism or anti-clericalism: 27 (including women) showed an interest in training for the diaconate. Some have received religious and priestly vocations. Many witnessed to a deeper love for the Eucharist and Mary.

Perhaps the most encouraging discovery was the response to the question requesting the recipient to state how he would explain the "baptism of the Spirit" to a non-Pentecostal. Not one paper confused this with the Sacrament of Baptism or mentioned tongues but most saw it as a release of the Spirit who was already given in the Sacraments of Baptism and Confirmation, a closer life with Jesus and the development of the fruits of the Spirit. There was no sign of elitism. The present writer intends to examine these findings more critically with the help of a sociologist but one difficulty arises from the fact that many groups do not invite scholarly research; many of the larger groups did not reply to the questionnaire.

Pentecostalism seems therefore to be an experience from which one gains a great deal but not one in which one should necessarily desire to stay. Indeed, if the "baptism of the Spirit" is a touch of infused contemplation it will come and go and it cannot be won or preserved by mere human efforts. The formation of tightly knit communities exclusively for those who have been baptized in the Spirit may well prevent the movement from sharing its blessings with the rest of the Church. It is noticeable that those groups associated with religious houses or trained personnel such as the Benedictines or the Dominicans are flourishing in a remarkable way. There will always be the tendency for the "enthusiasts" to live in an unreal dimension, to withdraw from the world and develop the features of a sect. In order to prevent this it seems that several things are necessary: they must be guided by the non-enthusiasts; they must show a deep social concern; have plenty of contact with non-Pentecostal Christians; exercise wide rotation of leadership; avoid large communities which will entail much organization and many rules; pursue intellectual studies and eschew para-ecclesial structure. It is also necessary that non-Pentecostal Christians join the prayer meetings and contribute by speaking and praying. Finally, the enthusiasm and faith of Pentecostals offers a challenge to the Church but enthusiasm itself also throws the gauntlet to professional people such as theologians, psychologists, sociologists and bishops. Can they by a patient and sympathetic understanding of Pentecostalism prevent it going "the way of all Charismatic Flesh" and integrate it with the twentieth-century Church?

Albert-Marie Besnard

The Influence of Asiatic Methods of Meditation

THERE ARE two main reasons for the increased interest shown in recent years by many Christians, including those in religious life, in the Eastern methods of meditation, in particular Yoga and Zen Buddhism.[1] The first is the increasingly felt need for an asceticism that will be re-educative and practicable in daily life. The second reason, which is of particular concern to us here, is the need to give prayer greater freedom and increased seriousness.

From this last point of view what Christians hope to gain from Yoga and from Zen can be summed up in a few words: they are looking for *the integration of the body into prayer*. It is obvious that the traditional forms of prayer cannot meet the challenge of the modern world and that Christians have to be present in the world and to others and therefore present to God through their bodies. There is, however, far more to this than just associating the body a little more closely with prayer. One of the first discoveries made by those initiated into Yoga and Zen is that the posture which is adopted (with all that this implies of rigour in maintaining it, perfection of relaxation, control of breathing,

[1] Yoga is, or rather Yogas are the disciplines practised in Hinduism, while Zen is connected with a form of Buddhism which flourished first in China, then reached Japan at the turn of the twelfth–thirteenth centuries. Although there is a fundamental relationship between these two disciplines, they are also notably different: Zen reduces the various asânas to one single sitting position (*zazen*) and the meditative walk (*kin-hin*) and its breathing and concentration practices are also more simple than those of Yoga. Other methods like "transcendental meditation" do not concern us here.

and so on) reveals and implants an attitude of integration of body and mind as regards reality, the life of the individual, and God for whom he is searching. It implies a far more decisive commitment to a spiritual way of life than is imagined by those who at first see only a more harmonious (or just a more comfortable!) way of praying.

The second necessity is silence or concentration. This is an urgent need at a time when too many voices are talking through too many interlocking channels, when this flood of talk becomes difficult to control, in which the individual can hardly hear the murmur of his own deepest existence, which alone assures him a consciousness of his identity. There is also a reaction against the verbiage which is rampant in the Church as well as elsewhere: those who want to pray, feel that neither the words nor the ideas convey the mystery and that a certain silence on the part of God, which they find painful, would perhaps give way to a perceptible word from him, if they themselves could only find the haven of a certain silence. For very many, the search for this silence is also the result of a doubt about the cogency of certain beliefs or the quality of their own faith: they need to be silent to give themselves a chance of being born into a new truth about themselves and their relationship with God. The Asiatic disciplines are able not only to contribute silence, but also to introduce the experience of non-duality (*advaita*). They can open up the sometimes fearful abysses of a vacuum or emptiness, of which the initiated Westerner at first suspects neither the depths nor the significance.

The integration of the body and the search for silence are a means to an end. What is finally envisaged is the bringing about of a *transformation of the personality* which realizes here and now the new dimensions of existence proposed by the Gospel. Just as the Hindu progresses towards the ecstasy of *samadhi*, or the Buddhist towards the illumination of *satori*, which are an intuitive experience of essential reality, in the same way the Christian who practises Yoga or Zen is motivated by the desire to realize something of the Christian experience presented to him by his faith: to meet God in truth, to allow the Spirit to transform him into a man of active justice and universal brotherhood, to

live with the life of the Trinity. Deep and increasing ignorance
of the different levels of consciousness and of the laws governing
them had led to a mistrust of personal experience by the Church,
since it was seen only in terms of a univocal and clearly suspect
subjectivism. Thus Catholicism tended to reduce the language of
Christian experience, till it was no more than a collection of
manners of speaking, the significance of which escaped the
majority of people. The result is that many people break away
from a faith, in which they see nothing but a very human system
of beliefs, of moral principles, and of social organization, all
now obsolete. But others have an intimation that the "knowledge of the Father and of his ambassador Jesus Christ", the life
according to the Spirit, the reconciliation between God and man,
in short the whole of the Gospel, are experiences to live as well as
statements to affirm. This being so, they then find themselves
abruptly facing a dual demand: that of "discerning spirits" or
establishing criteria of authenticity for experience; and that of the
dynamic relationship between this interiorized experience and an
active and responsible way of living in the world.

It will be readily admitted that any such enterprise would be
risky in the extreme without teachers qualified both by their
practice of Asiatic disciplines drawn from the best sources and
by their experience of its relationship to God according to the
Gospel. There is now beginning to be a nucleus of men who
fulfil these conditions. To cite some leading names among those
whose experience and writings are beginning to gain authority:
for Yoga, the Benedictines J. Dechanet[2] and H. Le Saux;[3] for Zen,
the Jesuits H. M. Enomiya-Lassalle[4] and W. Johnson.[5] It is also

[2] *Christian Yoga,* 1st edn 1960, paperback 1965; *Yoga in Ten Lessons*
(London, 1965); *Les Cahiers du Val* (quarterly, 38, Valjouffrey, France).
[3] *Sagesse hindoue, mystique chrétienne* (Paris, 1965; English trai s. Delhi,
1971); *Eveil à soi, éveil à Dieu* (Paris, 1971).
[4] *Zen—Way to Enlightenment* (London, 1967)· *Zen-Buddhismus*
(Cologne, 1966); *Zen Meditation für Christen* (Weilh. m, 1969). At the end
of 1969 Fr Lasalle founded a Catholic entre for Zen meditation not far
from Tokyo (cf. *Information Catholiques Internationales*, Paris, 15 May
1971, pp. 4-5).
[5] *The Still Point* (New York, 1970); *Christian Zen* (New York, 1971). In
Japan itself the Dominican N. Osmita and the Carmelite A. Okumura
should be mentioned (the latter has written *Le Zen: dépassement, presence
et liberté, Carmel* 49, La Plesse-Avrillé, Dec. 1970, pp. 262-75).

of interest to note that the famous Cistercian, the late Thomas Merton, was beginning to feel drawn to these questions.[6]

This development astonishes some and worries others. There is both opposition and mistrust. Without rejecting it completely, those who are antagonistic maintain there is a fundamental incompatibility between the principles of Christian mysticism, even apophatic, and Asiatic mysticism, for the first rests on the positive fact of the Incarnation and the objective ecstasy of love, not on the ecstasy of meditation.[7] In this last, is there not a dangerous obliteration of the dual I–thou relationship, which characterizes the originality of the connection between God and man in Revelation? Monoideism, the transcendence of all form, the silence of emptiness surely all involve the danger of forgetting the Word, the events of our salvation and Christian dogmas? To the authority of those who justify the Christian adaptation of these disciplines is opposed the authority of those, such as J. Monchanin, who admit to great reservations and who, while not completely excluding any recourse to such practices, fear, among other things, that they might "accustom people to doing without grace" and without God himself, that they would weaken the sense of sin, and that they would lead to a naturalistic quietism.[8]

We would propose the following possible points of agreement:

1. A statement of fact: the growing interest in Eastern methods of meditation denotes a new awareness among Christians of their legitimate needs (a balanced asceticism, prayer, contemplation), which the Church today finds it is in no position to satisfy.

2. If one is happy merely to carry out "gymnastic exercises, body positions and breathing controls, which constitute the elementary step of Yoga", with the object of "acquiring the physio-

[6] *Zen and the Birds of Appetite* (Abbey of Gethsemani, 1968), *Mystique et Zen* (Paris, 1972). It is impossible to cite here all those who have studied these problems specifically from a speculative point of view. Mention should be made at least of O. Lacombe, *Sarvâstivâdin* (Paris, 1956); H. Dumoulin, *Östliche Meditation und christliche Mystike* (Freiburg im Br., 1966); J. A. Cuttat, *Expérience chrétienne et spiritualité orientale* (Paris, 1967).

[7] For instance, J. Sudbrack, s.j., "Faszination aus dem Osten", *Geist und Leben*, Dec. 1971, pp. 424–79.

[8] See "Problèmes du Yoga chrétien", *Axes*, Oct.–Nov. 1969, pp. 19–31.

logical and psychological equilibrium indispensable to true prayer", there is no particular problem, but "this has nothing in fact to do with Yoga".[9]

3. On the other hand, if one penetrates deeply into the true logic of Yoga and Zen, the way of mental void and the experience of non-duality, then the fundamental question arises: is this an acceptable way for the Christian? Those who can speak with authority on the subject, because their knowledge is as much experimental as theological (e.g., Lassalle, Le Saux), give a positive answer subject to certain conditions. It seems to them that elements already inherent in the Christian tradition, for example in the mystics, of whom they have made a careful study, provide an answer to many of the objections which have been put forward.

The facts seem to indicate that there is, on the one hand, a growing awareness that something of the mystical experience, as it is called, should become the share of a more considerable number of the baptized, unless the salt of the Gospel is to lose its savour; and, on the other hand, that this experience, such as it has been lived up till now by a few isolated individuals, has for most of the time been either suspect or mistrusted or too superficially studied. That is why it is important that dialogue between those who have started to practise Yoga and Zen should be intensified and that some original thinking should be developed, so that there could be a simultaneous interaction between direct experience, a re-reading of the spiritual experiences of the Christian tradition, and a theology of Christian experience in general, integrating the fruits of the new studies of man himself, which our epoch can provide.

It is relevant to add that, although this is far from being a direct aim for the majority of new Christian adepts of Eastern methods of meditation, one of the fruits of these practices would probably be the opening up of a new opportunity for dialogue between Christianity, on the one hand, and Hinduism and Buddhism on the other.[10]

[9] H. Le Saux, *Sagesse hindoue, mystique chrétienne*, op. cit., p. 32.
[10] H. Dumoulin, "A Meeting with Zen-Buddhists", *Concilium*, Nov. 1967 (American edn Vol. 29). W. Johnston, "Dialogue with Zen", *Concilium*, Nov. 1969 (American edn Vol. 49); Vatican II, Decree on Non-Christian Religions, §2.

The question remains open, however, whether the West will succeed in developing its own Yoga or its own Zen (presuming this is at all meaningful). J. Dechanet hopes so: "There is little point in wresting Yoga practices from their Vedantic or Hindu matrix; we must assimilate them, make them part of our customs and, without doing violence to an art of living and a wisdom which does not belong to us, adapt the elements to our own way of life, our ideas, and our faith, to make a bond between its essence and our existence."[11]

APPENDIX

The following experiments, now taking place in various countries, give some idea of how these theories are being put into practice collectively in a specifically Christian context. In Germany during the past few years many "meditation" sessions (in the Zen style) have been led by Fr Emomiya-Lassalle or by Count K. von Dürckheim,[12] and these have rapidly gained followers. There is evidence of a growing interest in these sessions on the part of those in religious life, both contemplatives (notably Benedictines) and active religious, as well as those responsible for the education of priests.[13] In Belgium, at the abbey of Orval, and in France in several places, similar sessions have taken under the aegis of K. von Dürckheim and his assistants, and these have attracted laymen (especially doctors, teachers of Yoga and physical expression, and psychologists) as well as diocesan priests and men and women religious.[14] Taisen Deshimaru, a Japanese monk

[11] *Les Cahiers du Val, nom. cit.*, p. 103.
[12] Director of the centre for psychotherapy and encounter at Todtmoos-Rütte (Black Forest). Author of many works, among them *Le zen et l'Occident* (Bruxelles, 1962); *Pratique de la voie intérieure* (Paris, 1968). An essay by J. Lortz on theological implications arising out of K. von D.'s work can be found in *Auf dem Wege zum personalen Transzendenten, Transzendenz als Erfahrung* (Festschrift zum 70. Geburtstag von Graf Dürckheim) (Weilheim, 1966), pp. 237–50.
[13] See the account of a typical session in *Christ in der Gegenwart* (Freiburg-im-Br., 1971), No. 52, pp. 411–12. Among the abbeys open for such sessions are Königmünster and Münsterschwarzach.
[14] See the accounts of these sessions in A. Delaye, "Une session de méditation", *Carmel*, 49 La Plesse-Avrillé (France), June 1971, pp. 153–4. O. de Valence, "Zen et prière chrétienne", *La Maison-Dieu* No. 109 (1st quarter 1972).

of the Soto Zen school who has worked in Paris since 1967, has seen his contacts with Catholic circles multiply, particularly with religious.[15] For Yoga, which has had a longer history in the West, an attempt is under way to bring together in a centre for research all those who are in agreement with this statement of intent: "... to find the norms of a healthy Yoga, which respects the essence (human and spiritual) of this ancient discipline, but adapted to our lives and, above all, to our way of and attitude to life (*Weltanschauung*)".[16] In Sweden, in view of the success of the initial experiments, a Carmelite and a university professor are opening a "centre for meditation" at Rättvick. In the United States some original experiments have been tried: Yoga retreats, ecumenical meetings under the auspices of these disciplines, the establishment of "houses of prayer" (especially in the Detroit area), and so on.[17]

Translated by Rosaleen Ockenden

[15] Cf. J.-M. Petit, "Dialogue entre le bouddhisme zen et le carmel", in *Carmel*, March 1970, pp. 74–7.
[16] *Les Cahiers du Val*, No. 17 (Oct.–Dec. 1971), p. 103.
[17] G. A. Maloney, "And Now, the Yoga Retreat", *America*, 5 June 1971, pp. 591–3; B. Häring, "A Contemplative House", *Rev. for Religious*, Sept. 1967; Sr Ann Chester IHM, "Report on Hope 1970", *Sisters Today*, Dec. 1970.

Joseph Beaude

Mysticism and Poetry in Seventeenth-Century France

IT IS impossible to present in a few pages the whole panorama of mystical poetry in France in the seventeenth century. From Claude Hopil to Mme Guyon there is abundant evidence of a flourishing literary genre, which would rightly be the subject of a lengthy study. It is true that I ought to define precisely what is meant by mysticism, and so to limit the scope of mystical poetry. But this reduction of mystical poetry to a few exemplary works would demand a theoretical justification which would range too widely and so extend far beyond the limits of a short article. Let us therefore agree, in spite of the reference to a multiplicity of texts that this implies, to understand the term "mystical" in a fairly wide and general sense and to some extent to identify "mystical poetry" with "spiritual poetry". It is therefore relevant to emphasize first and foremost the abundance and variety of spiritual poems. A brief presentation of the various poetical forms and themes will follow, with particular reference to the first third of the seventeenth century. Then a more detailed review of the attraction felt by poets of the time to the figure of Mary Magdalen will allow light to be shed on some aspects of the mystical lyricism of the period.

In French poetic literature of the sixteen-hundreds, religious poetry occupies a position of the first importance. The poets most read at the time, those whose names recur most frequently in anthologies, for example, are Desportes, Bertaut and Du Perron. The first undertook, in his old age, to translate the 150 psalms into verse. The other two were converted by the Counter-

Reformation movement, became princes of the Church and abandoned amorous verses for biblical paraphrases, spiritual canticles and prayers. But the poetry of these quasi-official writers is "more a political than a mystical instrument". Very different and, at all events, less political, more spontaneous and more sincere is the poetry of many poets, men or women, Catholic or Huguenot, who have no literary fame. They wrote an exclusively devotional poetry, that is, they made the language of poetry their language of meditation and their prayer.

It is in the course of the second half of the sixteenth century that poetry of devotion developed. But its themes show an evolution. The poets of the same generation as Jean de Sponde, who died in 1595 and who is known for his fine *Méditations sur les Pseaumes* and *Poèmes Chrétiens*, meditated on death and spoke of penitence. At the beginning of the seventeenth century poetry offers many points of interest. If the theme of death still recurs frequently, it is no longer, as in Sponde's works, in the form of an intimate meditation on the precariousness of life here and the desire for a life in the future, but rather in the form of a bloody and cruel spectacle calculated to arouse strong and violent feelings. Christ's Passion was one of the chosen subjects. The scenes are described with colour and realism. The poet then takes over the mystery and makes it his own, unites his pain with the sufferings of the crucified Christ, suffering of which he as a sinner is the cause and as a redeemed man the beneficiary. This is the course taken by the meditation which we find in the *Théorèmes sur le sacré Mystère de nostre Rédemption*, the first volume of which appeared in 1613, the second, consecrated in its turn to the glorious mysteries, in 1622. The *Théorèmes* are, in the etymological sense of the term, visions or contemplations. Jean Rousset[1] has noted the Ignatian influence on the *Théorèmes*: there is true "composition of place", the presentation of the mystery to the imagination. The sonnets of La Ceppède, which he himself often called meditations, are real "spiritual exercises". For his part, La Ceppède, who sprinkled his poems with numerous references, frequently quoted not only the Fathers of

---

[1] Jean Rousset, *L'intérieur et l'extérieur. Essais sur la poésie et sur le théatre au XVIIe siècle* (Paris, 1968), p. 30, which reprints Rousset's preface to an edition of the *Théorèmes* of La Ceppède.

the Church but the Carthusian Ludolphe and after him more recent authors such as Guevara, Louis of Granada or Diego of Estella. These all possess a spirituality both concrete and full of images. The authors of "lives of Christ" or "books of Calvary" are favourite sources. Devotional poetry is centred above all on the scenes and tableaux of the life of Christ. The word "mystery" is used therefore in the sense of representation, in the same way as one talks of the "mysteries" of the Rosary. The joyous mysteries are not entirely absent, the Nativity among others keeps its place, but it is above all the contemplation of the sorrowful mysteries that is dominant.

The poetic meditations of La Ceppède aim at "compassion", at participation in the mystery of redemption. The works of his contemporaries or successors do not all have the spiritual and theological vigour of his writing. In many writers sentimentality predominates, their works offer a poetry of emotion and tears. César de Nostredame, son of the celebrated Nostradamus and compatriot and friend of La Ceppède, evoked in his work not the suffering Christ but the great "lamenters": the plaintive Virgin, Mary Magdalen, the good thief; and Auvray in his *Pourmenade de l'âme dévote*, a "way of the cross", described the tortures and death of Christ with exacerbated expressionism to excite violent feelings and pity in the soul of the reader. Of great significance in this respect is the fact that one of the liturgical chants most frequently put into verse was the *Stabat Mater*.

Although the importance accorded by poets to the sorrowful mysteries had to be emphasized, spiritual poetry is more than just a "mystique" of the Passion. One greatly favoured genre is the paraphrase of biblical texts and especially of the psalms. There are numerous translations of the psalter into French verse. Finally and above all, there is that poetry to which in all justice the name "mystical" must be accorded. The great exponent of this genre was Claude Hopil, whose main work, *Les Divins eslancemens d'amour exprimez en cent cantiques faits en l'honneur de la Tres-Saincte Trinité* (1629), was no longer imagination and vision of the mysteries, but contemplation of *the* Mystery. In it is expressed a mysticism of night, of holy and learned ignorance. To contemplate the Mystery is, according to Hopil, "to see without seeing". The soul stands before the incomprehensible, which is the divine being, and is only united to the divine by its lack of knowledge, by a "sovereign death", a "mystical decease". It is a poetry of light and of darkness, of a darkness which is light.

Such a compressed picture can give but a very imperfect idea of spiritual poetry at the beginning of the seventeenth century. To escape from generalities, let us consider a few more detailed reflections on Mary Magdalen, a figure sung and celebrated as no other at that time.

The literature on the subject of Magdalen is in fact extremely copious in the seventeenth century, as much in prose as in poetry. Poetry does not always shine in verses—as Goujet says in his *Bibliothèque Française* (1740) on the subject of the interminable epics on Magdalen—which are often extravagant and trivial, for instance those of Remy de Beauvais, *La Magdeleine* (1617) and of F. M. Durant, *La Magdeliade* (1622).

Hardly any of this literature has in fact come down to posterity. Nevertheless, the presence in the culture of the time of the figure of the converted sinner, of the lover of Christ, of the recluse of the Holy Balm—these are the titles which gain her the favour of the poets—must have a significance. It is worth trying to isolate a few of the reasons for the attention given at the time to this figure from the gospels.

One of the essential themes evoked by the figure of Magdalen is that of absence. She suffers the absence of Christ—at the foot of the Cross, at the empty tomb, in the desert of Provence. But precisely this absence is a grace. It is the prerequisite of desire, of the growth of love: "You flee her a while to rekindle the embers: As a little cold water makes the furnace burn more brightly, A little absence makes friendship blaze" (La Ceppède).

Love increased by absence is certainly a constant theme of literature, of philosophy and of spiritual theology. But it is valid to ask whether in fact it was only so greatly valued in the seventeenth century because absence is something experienced by so many. Christ no longer speaks. What this means is that in spite of appearances, in spite of the affirmations of a devout humanism, in which religious poetry to a great extent shares, an uncertainty lies heavily upon Christian language. Magdalen comes to give an example of faith in uncertainty, of Jesus' gift of love even from far off, of God's presence even at an insuperable distance. In short, the presentation of Magdalen, even in the least mystical of the poets, comes down to a sort of vulgarization of mystical themes called, despite everything, to the rescue of faithfulness amid the overthrow of so many certainties. Fideism was common at that time and Magdalen was in some way the guarantee, the archetype of faith kept, love given, absence endured. Fideism and mysticism are perhaps related, the first being the incomplete and abortive skeleton of the second. The seventeenth century was a time when both flourished.

The language used by the poets about Magdalen is ambiguous. It is, as we have noted, sometimes trivial, but even in the poems of the most elevated and spiritual writers the love-songs of this converted woman to the divine lover surely remain equivocal. The sinner Magdalen fascinates as much as Magdalen the saint. The prostitute is inseparable from the follower of Jesus. In this the character is in keeping with the baroque themes of masks, ambiguity and metamorphosis. She is also a typical character in a poetic literature which surprises us by its juxtaposition, in the works of the same poet, of licentious evocations and the most fervent prayers.

Is this deliberate in an age when religion has so strong a hold? The question is perhaps not so simple and cannot be put in these terms. The libertine jeers at morality, but so does the mystic in his fashion. A puritanical faith is either hypocritical, or disembodied, or suspected of angelism. To make a distinction between Eros and Agape does not mean to separate them. The Magdalenian fervour of the seventeenth century would give psychiatrists something to think about. It also gives plenty of cause for thought to the historian of ideas. The period was, it seems, one of those in which the tension between the two loves was simultaneously of the most violent and the most fraternal sort. Magdalen is the figure of wild and divine desire. She is presented as one whose fever becomes fervour, whose lack of satisfaction becomes redemptive deprivation, whose loss becomes salvation. Only because she "had loved greatly" could she become this suffering but pacified lover in the desert of the Holy Balm. She it is who sees the mystery of God not through the eyes of her intelligence but, as Hopil says, through the eyes of love, crucifying love: "Michael the Archangel has put a cross in the cave and you see God's paradise in that beautiful mirror."

*   *   *   *

Only rarely in the history of Christianity has there been such a number of spiritual poets as at the end of the sixteenth and the beginning of the seventeenth century. There are many possible explanations of this frequent recourse to poetry to express faith. The apologetic reasons so often given by the authors of the period, who want to take issue with the secular poets, are unconvincing. The predominance of a symbolic way of thinking in pre-Cartesian culture must have played a part. It was, in addition, a time when contrasts and contradictions were not only not reduced but accentuated and enjoyed. The Christian faith itself is made up of shadow and light. The language of poetry is precisely the most apt language to express tensions without resolving them. And it seems, in fact, to be one of the essential characteristics of this poetry that the Christian soul can speak and sing in it both sorrowfully and happily, in confusion or in confidence, incarnate or divine. One might say that the mystery of the Incarnation, which allies paradoxically man and God, is the most apposite for this baroque age of antinomical alliances: in the soft flesh of the poetic word the word of God speaks out.

Translated by Rosaleen Ockenden

Bruno Borchert

The Jesus Movement

AS FAR as spirituality is concerned, the Jesus Movement was undoubtedly one of the most significant events of last year. What did in fact take place? Having studied most of the available material, I have come to the conclusion that a cover story in *Time* (21 June 1971) was decisive in setting this movement afoot. It had previously been reported quite widely in the world press, but this cover story was followed by a flood of publicity in the English-speaking world.

What the *Time* article did was to bring all the different movements together and present them as a single movement of revolution in the sub-culture of young people, who were turning away from sex and drugs and Eastern spirituality and towards the traditional, Western, Christian culture of Jesus, the One Way.

This Jesus Revolution, however, was to a great extent a revival of the Pentecostal movement, not only on the fringe of Protestantism, but also underground in the Roman Catholic Church. Such revivals form part of the American religious tradition. Neither they nor the growing interest in Jesus of Nazareth among artists and ordinary people outside the churches, atheists and even Jews as well as biblical scholars are in any way new or revolutionary in the strict sense of the word. The questions that are above all being asked by older as well as younger people are, for example, who was this man, Jesus of Nazareth, how did he live, what did he want to do and why did he have such an influence? The image of Jesus that is being discovered is that of a socially engaged man.

The real revolutionaries are perhaps the so-called Jesus freaks, who combine elements of the sub-culture with an extremely conservative form of Christianity, seeing Jesus as a living God, both saviour and judge, the one who determines the fate of man. Jesus guides every human action and solves every problem. Man's life must be governed by an intense personal relationship with this Jesus and as a result many Jesus freaks live in communes reminiscent of the strict monastic communities of the past.

The Rev. Edward E. Plowman, the "historian of the Jesus movement" according to *Time*, believes that this Jesus movement began with the love movement in the Haight-Ashbury district of San Francisco in the summer of 1967. Father Harris, the parish priest of this district, believes that the hippie culture is probably closer than any other today to primitive Christianity. Genuine hippies, he maintains, really practise love, a selfless *agape* in the Pauline sense. They protest against selfish parents who boast that they are monogamous, but practise progressive polygamy by divorcing again and again, against the contradiction between moral pronouncements and moral practice, against the conviction that financial success is a sign of God's favour. This, Father Harris believes, is why they turn away from the Church as they see it and its *mystique*—a popular word among hippies. Father Harris is, however, convinced that genuine hippies have direct experience of God, whether they use drugs or not, and that they undoubtedly pass the test of mystical experience, which is, does it lead to a better way of life or does it increase love and understanding?

This love movement spread very quickly and was soon joined by displaced young people coming from all over the United States. It was also to some extent distorted by publicity, so that, by October 1967, the genuine hippie ideal was almost dead.

Like the underground Pentecostal movement in Roman Catholicism, which emerged at about the same time, this Jesus movement continued quietly, but it can hardly be identified with the so-called Jesus people, although they were grouped together as one in the *Time* article. The term seems to include a number of different movements. The Children of God are fundamentalist, strict and exclusive, apocalyptic and remote from the world. The Process combines Jesus with Satan. The Way sees prosperity and luxury as a sign of faith in Jesus. What have all these different Jesus movements in common? They do not belong to any one Church. They are above all movements and rather unpredictable and difficult to define. Finally, they all confess, in one way or another, one or another Jesus.

What has survived of this Jesus revolution? Above all, I think, the ways in which the "sub-culture" expresses itself, especially through the mass media, have changed. This is clear from the use of special clothes, symbols, slogans, music, stickers and posters and the development of the underground press, festivals and shows. In this sub-culture, the psychedelic element has become a "Jesus kick"—Jesus is the best trip; Jesus makes me high. It provides young people with a new way of expressing their religiosity without sex and drugs. What is very difficult to establish is the extent to which this way of life is determined by publicity and advertising or by commercial manipulation, and thus, ultimately, by older people, and the extent to which it originates among the young people themselves. That manipulation plays a part cannot be disputed—I would call *Jesus Christ Superstar* an example of this. The première on Broadway was dominated by a not particularly religious élite to the accompaniment of protests on the part of Jesus freaks. Its success, moreover, is certainly to a great extent due to excellent promotion by Robert Stigwood, the promotor of *Oh, Calcutta!*, in London and Tom O'Horgan, the promoter of *Hair*, on Broadway. (The commercial manipulation of the Jesus movement has been discussed in detail in an article in *Der Spiegel*, 14 February 1972.) There is every reason to suspect that the whole business of sacrality within criticism of society has in fact been thought up by the establishment and supported by it.

The publicity given to the Jesus movement has provided it with an exceptional opportunity to develop in a special direction and the image of Jesus promoted by the mass media has, of course, been that of a sweet, unhistorical, long-haired Jesus. This version of the Jesus movement first of all fits very well into the American tradition of popularizing artistic representations of what is easily recognizable and at the same time often false and sentimental. Secondly, it also fits into the traditional popular devotion to a similarly falsified and sentimentalized Jesus (or saint)

This type of devotion either takes all the shocking elements out of any figure who might otherwise disturb the established order or the passive submissiveness of the people and thus raises him to the altar or else roundly declares him to be heretical. What has long been appreciated by the world of commerce is that frustrated commitment is followed by a vacuum that can easily be filled by a supraterrestrial, sweetly religious stimulus which is suitable for all ages. The smoke screen of commercial publicity is always threatening to obscure the constant element of religious experience or at least of longing for mystical experience that is present in the sub-culture of youth and the fact that both the secular and the religious establishments have disclaimed this quest. It would not be going too far to say that, after a short period of hope during the pontificate of John XXIII and the Council, the Roman Catholic Church has returned—permanently, so it would seem—to the old tradition of safe popular devotion and of strenuous disapproval of everything to do with real or mystical experience.

Only the future will show to what extent this Jesus movement of commercial publicity will take root. Its manifestation is different, for example, in the United States and in Germany, where it has gained ground impressively under the influence of American methods of publicity and under the leadership of, among others, Rev. Volkhard Spitzer in Berlin, who claims that the German Jesus people are less emotional and wildly enthusiastic than their counterparts in America. Spitzer belongs, strictly speaking, to a Pentecostal community, but aims to get the Jesus people movement off the ground as an independent movement directed especially towards drug addicts and those seeking sexual experiences. Commercial interests have, of course, been playing a decisive part in shaping this movement in Germany.

What is the situation in the Netherlands? Certainly, anything that happens in the United States seems always to happen very soon afterwards in Holland, but there is inevitably a difference in the part played by commercial publicity, which seems to function more as a means of spreading information. As early as 1967, members of a Pentecostal movement were trying to help young people to give up drugs, and with some success. The Jesus movement is really, in a sense, a new ingredient in the hotch-potch that Holland has been for years and that Amsterdam is now *par excellence*. The best ingredient in this international hotchpotch is, I believe, the growing emphasis on meditation, which is not thrust aside by other religious movements, but which rather absorbs them. The best known centre of meditation is Cosmos in Amsterdam, but similar phenomena can be found all over the Netherlands, where people are finding "Jesus" better than LSD.

Looked at from a distance, the Jesus revolution as a world event tends to give a rather pale impression, compared with the phenomenal growth in industrialized society of occultism, white witchcraft and astral religions, for example, and the rapid emptying of the established churches.

We may conclude, I think, with a very relevant question. Has it not become increasingly clear in recent years that the spirituality of contemporary man, whose life is so influenced by technological developments, has been moving farther and farther away from that provided by the official churches and is the Jesus movement not simply one aspect of this world event?[1]

[1] My main source of information has been the material available at the Titus Brandsma Institute at Nijmegen; see my acknowledgment in *Speling*, 1972, No. 1, which was devoted to the subject of ecstasy and in which sources of information about the sub-culture of youth and the revival of religiosity in general will be found.

Translated by David Smith

Gérard Bessière

Do Revolutionaries Pray?
Testimonies from South America

A NUMBER of collective or individual replies from Colombia, Bolivia, Brazil, Uruguay and Chile to the question "Do revolutionaries pray?" form the basis of this article, in which I have not mentioned names or countries, but have tried to provide an overall impression. Seen as a whole, the replies are, I think, representative, even though it was impossible to take a satisfactory sample. But first of all, *what is meant by the words "revolutionaries" and "prayer"?* Several replies stressed—"You must define which 'revolution' you mean and, if prayer has some connection with God, which 'God' you mean."

The word revolution has acquired such prestige that everybody wants to be thought of as "revolutionary", and every change and every nonconformist attitude is described as "revolutionary". As for the word "God", its content is relative to the "ideal image that one has of one's personal life and of life in society" and the idea that the revolutionary has of "prayer" depends greatly on this. "Theological symbols" are similarly socially conditioned. The "official" Church and its theology, including that of Vatican II, are "tied to capitalist society".

A revolutionary can be regarded as "any person committed to the transformation of society", but "it is difficult to define what a committed Christian is". A former leader of Catholic Action at the university level replied: "There are two kinds of revolutionary Christian. Some work in groups and therefore live in more intense dialogue with the Lord. Revolutionary Christians of the second type are also committed, but live more in isolation, with their own personal vitality. Their prayer is more spasmodic, less systematic, and it may be more or less rich."

Commitment is a change of attitude. "Revolutionary commitment means the abandonment of everything that is traditional and institutional, all connection with the comfortable world. One loses one's original point of reference in prayer." It is almost always accompanied by a break with the Church. "Many of those who are involved in revolutionary politics are young people who were trained in Catholic Action and almost all of them broke with the Church as soon as they became politically active. Many of the political prisoners at Recife are young people and they say that they are no longer Christians." Young people who become politically committed are abandoning not only the institutional Church, but also their own Christian communities. "Why?"

There is also a break with traditional prayer. "When you change your way of acting in the world, you also change your way of expressing your spirituality. You drop traditional prayer such as The Lord's Prayer and you look for other ways of communicating with God. Prayer can no longer be institutional— you pray much more in action. As an individual, you pray in the middle of your daily activity, for example, before a meeting, but it is difficult to pray alone, without a group. Many people replace prayer by revolutionary mysticism, which is not merely concrete action, but also a commitment lived at a very profound level."

What is rejected is prayer which withdraws from action. "Marxists—former Christians—criticize us for praying, because they see it as dependence upon 'God', and as a failure to recognize man's own capabilities. For them, prayer is alienation, escapism." Hence the saying: "Yesterday we prayed, today we have to act." Others say: "We will talk about prayer when a solution has been found for an urgent problem."

Many say that they are looking for a new kind of prayer, new ways of praying, of facing up to the Gospel and the urgent situations which make demands upon them. They say, for example, "active commitment on behalf of others, under the impulse of love, is prayer". They look for "the prayer which commits you, strengthens you and gives you courage".

Many replies emphasize the effectiveness of prayer in moments of danger, the loneliness of action and the discovery of one's limitations. "Is this a purely psychological process or the action of the Holy Spirit in me?" This was the question asked by one man who found strength after an hour of prayer, one day when he found himself alone after his companion in the struggle had defected. "In concrete action with others, you discover your limitations and weaknesses, and prayer is an attempt to seek the strength to overcome these limitations." "Prayer is communication with Someone who can release us from tensions. This need for prayer is found in moments of difficulty and in moments of joy."

The relationship between prayer and action is mentioned again and again. "Prayer gives me a greater confidence in what I do in my everyday life." "My prayer is very simple: thanksgiving, reflection sometimes or sometimes quite simply being quiet. . . ." "In the past our prayer was asking for things, but now we have a prayer which is devoted more to thanksgiving; it is a more courageous and optimistic prayer." "Now prayer is more a source of energy for action. In the past we prayed not to fall or to ask forgiveness; now it is more positive—we ask to be firm and committed."

There is a frequent connection between *prayer and the group.* "Participating in a group helps you to pray. Prayer shared by members of the group allows them to have more profound human relationships in their lives." The reading of the Gospel with those who live in their part of the town "reveals the value of prayer", one activist of the extreme left in Chile, who lives with two companions in the middle of a working-class population, wrote, "Commitment leads Christians to look for new forms of life— communal life, new types of relationship between themselves. These lead to new forms of prayer."

A priest, a student chaplain, replied: "I am the one least committed, but who prays most, and my prayer serves the others who are revolutionary activists. People are always coming to ask me to pray with them. They look for and know where to find the Eucharist. Sometimes it is the person you least expected who comes."

Prayer often appeals to the Bible. "Reading the Bible is essential to prayer. The Word of the Bible is always modern and reading it makes it easier to give action a deep and convincing meaning." Many of the young political prisoners in Brazil who used to be members of Catholic Action, but say they are no longer Christians, "ask for a Bible to be brought".

Prayer is "direct dialogue with Christ—the Virgin and the saints seem to have lost ground". This direct relationship with Christ is a reflection of an attitude: "the integration of the presence of Another Person, the Lord, into all that I do. The Lord is with me throughout the day. This implies a change of attitude, leading to a readiness to give, to receive, to accept different points of view. In this way, the 'ethereal' Christ becomes a man who shares my life. Prayer is no longer static, fixed formulas said at set times, but dynamic. This is the prayer which inspires action." (An activist of the extreme left.) "I have a new image of Jesus. I pray to a different Jesus from the one I prayed to before. In the past I saw Jesus more as endowed with supernatural power, but now I have a more human image of Jesus. I respect him and love him more." (A communist active in Chile.) "We have left the Christ who, we thought, spoke individually to us, and we have gone over to a Christ who talks to us all as one man." (An activist journalist of the extreme left, Chile.)

A particularly moving testimony of this faith in Christ is to be found in the letters of Nestor Paz, who died in the Bolivian National Liberation Army: "My beloved Lord, it is a very long time since I have written to you. Today I really feel that I need you and your presence. Perhaps it is because death is close and the struggle has been relatively unsuccessful. You know that I have always sought, in every way, to be faithful to you. Fully consistent with myself. That is why I am here. Love, for me, is an urgent need to find a solution for the problems of my fellow men, within whom *you* live. I have left what I had and have come. Perhaps today is my Maundy Thursday and tomorrow night my Good Friday. I deliver what I am wholly into your hands, with unlimited confidence, because I love you. What hurts me is to leave what I love most, Ceci my wife and my family, and not be able to reach out and touch the triumph of the people, their liberation. We are a group filled with Christian and human fullness. That is enough, I think, to carry history forward. This comforts me. I love you and give you what I am and what we are, without limits, because you are my Father. No death is useless if life has been filled with meaning; and that is true, I believe, here with us.

"So long, Lord, till your heaven comes, the new earth for which we long so much. Francisco."

Can we come to any conclusion? If some "revolutionaries" abandon certain forms of prayer or give up praying, others work out, personally and in groups, a new prayer, within their own commitment, a prayer that is overflowing with life.

A young Christian worker, after having just escaped arrest while sticking up posters during the night in a street in Montevideo, wrote to God on her return home: "Father, as day is dawning, I want to talk to you about what I have just been through and say thank you, because it came out all right." She describes what she had been doing, the arrival of the police and her flight. She tells how she overcame her fear: "I was afraid, but I thought of you, poor Christ, who were despised, persecuted and crucified by the powerful men of that time because you lived with the poor, set free the oppressed and proclaimed the good news to everyone." She also says what she thinks about her people, conditioned by propaganda, for young people with no future, for activists of all sorts who are trying to build up a new world for man to live in. And she concludes: "Father, your Son gave us liberty so that we could be free. We will not be the slaves of other men. For this, I offer you my everyday life; your will be done."

The reply of a Brazilian bishop presents the two choices faced by the committed Christian: "There are two distinct forms of Christian life. Christians who are brought face to face with the need for revolutionary action, but have been brought up with a traditional relationship with God and a traditional model of Church and prayer are confronted with a choice. They must either find a new and deeper way of expressing their faith and their communion with God, or else give all this up, and it seems to me that this is what often happens. Many young revolutionaries either live without any explicit faith or else redefine what man is before God, before Christ and before the Church, in a concrete faith. One said to me that he lives unceasingly before God by carrying out his call to political commitment."

HEAR MY PRAYER
Psalm 5

"Hear my words, O Lord,
Hear my groaning,
Hear my protest.
For you are not a God who is a friend of dictators,
You are not a supporter of their politics,
Propaganda doesn't influence you."

> E. Cardenal, "Cri", *Psaumes politiques*,
> p. 11. Les Editions du Cerf, 1970.

Translated by R. A. Wilson

PART III
DOCUMENTATION
CONCILIUM

Pierre-Reginald Cren

Krishna's Flute

ONLY one language, poetry, could do justice to the naïve, creative
experience with which this article will be concerned. We shall
make do, however, with a sort of provisional prosaic account in
the margins of the still unwritten poem. Those who think they
have worked out once and for all the normative theoretical structure of the encounter between Christianity and the "non-Christian" religions in precise and careful terms should read no further, unless they can sense the power of spiritual discovery, even
in this field, to break in one day, like a gift as indisputable as it
is irresistible, and open doors which had been declared closed.
"You do not know the way of the wind" (Eccles. 11. 3).

A few months ago a Western Christian was travelling through
India, as many do. He was a professional theologian, and his
main interest was to discover the place of the other religions, and
especially Hinduism, in the plan of God. India was not at all for
him the scene of an unformed and ambiguous mystical search,
based on a vague or esoteric knowledge of Indian religions; it
was much more the testing-ground of knowledge acquired in
advance from a reading of the ancient texts and the study of the
works of Western orientalists.

One day, however, he was driven to Vrindaban, one of the
most famous centres of pilgrimage in Northern India.[1] It is here
that the tradition of the worship of Krishna, the Bhagavata

[1] A useful help to understanding the position and atmosphere of
Vrindaban is K. Klostermaier, *Hindu and Christian in Vrindaban* (London, 1969).

Purana in particular, places the episodes in the youth of the god Krishna in which the young herdsman captivated the shepherd-esses, the *gopis*, with the sound of his flute and played the game of love with them. But for the faithful Vrindaban is far from being just the evocation of a vanished past; it is the scene, carnal and mystical at once, of a mystery beyond time which ceaselessly unfolds there to the delight of the lovers of God. Vrindaban is, as it were, the sacramental land where Krishna and Radha, his be-loved *gopi*, are always present as a jubilant and none the less intimate manifestation of divine love.

The little town was calm; it was not the time of the great fes-tivals. But the rhythmic recitation of the names of God and the mystical chants never stops at Vrindaban. Our traveller was in-vited one day to attend a *Krishnalila*, in the inner courtyard of a private house, and so it was that every afternoon for several days he was an attentive spectator at the "game of Krishna", in which carefully chosen and rehearsed children act scenes from the Krishna legend and represent, in poetry, dancing and drama, various aspects of the single mystery of love. There are exuberant and popular *Krishnalilas*, but this one had a more intimate and contemplative character. It was also much more than a spectacle; it was a celebration. During the few hours for which the "game" lasted the children who took the parts of Krishna and Radha were not only the interpreters of a sacred story; they were a real presence of the young god with the flute and his beloved, who is nothing other than the god's own beauty made manifest. This was the message of the worship paid at the beginning and end of the "game" to the children who were for a time the symbolic incarnation of Krishna and Radha. It was also shown by the unique atmosphere of loving devotion with which the "perform-ance" was surrounded.

It is difficult to explain exactly what happened to the foreigner who came regularly to watch the sacred game. What is certain is that gradually, without consciously willing it and perhaps as a result of an availability without presuppositions and without reservations, he ceased to be a mere spectator and, literally, "en-tered into the game". He no longer went to the *lila* as to an exotic theatrical production which would give him a more direct appreciation of the "other". He began to attend it as a religious festival which involved him personally and which he experienced as a genuine movement of grace within which God was making himself known. Astonishing as it might have seemed to him before, the love of God revealed in Jesus Christ shone for him in the faces of Krishna and Radha. At first he regarded their "game" as a sort of parable, to which Christian faith gave him the key. But there was something much more important than this intellectual recognition. The experience was of a different order; it was an actual encounter, beyond doubt for the one who experienced it, with divine grace through the intermediary of this *Krishnalila*. One evening in particular, when at the end of the "performance" Radha presented him before the assembly with the wreath of white flowers which decorated her diadem, he was struck by the overwhelming realization that this gesture, which he might have considered as no more than an act of courtesy towards a guest and friend—which he also was—had a totally different dimension. It took its place, *hic et nunc*, in a sacramental process which was not at all the same as Christian sacramentality in the strict sense and could not replace it, but which was nevertheless not strange to him. It was as though the same supernatural history of salvation which was concentrated and fulfilled to its highest degree in Jesus Christ could adopt related signs, no doubt lower or subordinate but nevertheless real, which went beyond the doctrinally accepted limits.

There was certainly something unusual in the fact of a Christian's becoming, without denying anything of his recognition of Christ as God, but from the very heart of that recognition, a worshipper of Krishna, who had become for him a sort of mediation of the Christic reality itself. Like the *gopis* of the tradition, this stranger had heard the sound of Krishna's flute and had been seduced by that gentle music. He remembered the poems of Toukaram: "He who stands upright, his hands on his haunches and his body shining with a diffused light, he is the one who penetrates everything while remaining far away and distant.... He has become sensible for us, and it is a joy for his own to be able to love him, says Touka." And again: "My dark god [the word Krishna means 'dark'] has taken the face of a graceful, naked child.... Hands on his haunches, naïve and silent, standing, he waits for our love.... Though his home is in paradise,[2] says Touka, he also lives among his own." These poems, however, were no longer for him simply the attractive expression of an unusual form of worship. They now become part of his own praise of the Son, "the heir of all things (who) reflects the glory of God and bears the very stamp of his nature" (Heb. 1. 2–3). They now belonged, in their own place and without confusion, to the jubilant litany of the names of God and his manifestations; with the maratha pilgrim he could now chant, "Royal one, with childlike grace, living image of love".

This experience is offered for the comments of theologians. It is unarmed before their gaze; its only defence against suspicions of all sorts—syncretism, mental confusion, emotional illusion— is its solid certainty, reinforced however by the witness of a few Christian brothers buried in India who have gone through similar experiences. But the experience has a power of its own; at least for those to whom it has been given or who, from outside, feel its truth, it is a boulder against which the over-simple categories developed by theology to defend, rightly, the unique Lordship of Christ shatter. Does this mean that such an experience, of its nature, cannot be captured in the language of theologians? But in that case would not such a language, which was content not to pick up at its own level the lessons of spiritual experience, be no more than trendy gossip about isolated religious concepts? The most distressing feature of the present situation, to my mind, is that experiences of the sort we have described are probably made in a way "inadmissible" in the strict sense, not only because of their intimate nature—which would be understandable—but as the result of a prior theoretical repression. For a Christian to admit to being a worshipper of Krishna is a scandal in itself, shakes the most solid official foundations, is a paradigm error, one which confuses the fixed boundaries on the maps of official knowledge. Thus it is possible to meet Christians in India who must keep silent about the deepest level of their contemplation, through the religious signs of the country, of the universal mystery of Christ, under pain of becoming suspect in their own faith. No doubt mystics have always had more or less the same experi-

[2] Cf. Toukaram, *Psaumes du Pèlerin*, trad. G. A. Deleury (Paris, 1956), pp. 58–60, 146.

ence throughout the history of the Church. Of course precautions
are necessary, especially in an Indian context, where syncretism
is a permanent feature. The language of a particular spiritual
experience is not immediately universalizable, especially when
the experience takes place in an unfamiliar setting. Because this
language has the ambiguous plasticity of poetry, it needs to explain itself, or at least to defend itself, in an atmosphere of trust.

Our present story could, for example, be taken as meaning
that for our Christian worshipper of Krishna Krishna and Christ
are one, that they are thus interchangeable divine manifestations,
and that therefore Christ is of no benefit to the worshipper of
Krishna and that, more generally, in relation to salvation the
Christian and the Krishnaite in their different contexts are in an
identical situation. This, however, was precisely not the experience we have been describing. Our traveller saw the light of
Christ shining in the face of Krishna because he already recognized Christ by faith as Lord. He recognized in the game of love
of Krishna and Radha a parable and a quasi-sacrament of the
covenant between God and man only because he had received
from Christ the revelation of this covenant. In the Indian tradition, from the Bhagavad Gita on, there are many other images
of Krishna which left him indifferent or repelled him, but the
Krishna of this experience, the Krishna of the contemplative
bhakti which had given rise to the "game" of which he had been
the spectator, was not Christ, though he was a god of love incarnate among men to save them by grace and asked only the
allegiance of their love.[3] But he was, both imperfectly and with a
mysterious force, a figure who announced and mediated Christ,
a figure still veiled for the Hindu worshipper, but now revealed
for the Christian worshipper of the same Krishna.

There can be no doubt that the deepest level of the encounter
between Christianity and the other religions takes place in experiences of this kind, whether or not in the context of Krishna.

[3] This idea of a (multiple) "descent" by a God for the salvation of mankind is expressed, as is well known, in the Indian concept of the *avatar*.
This concept is complex, however, and varies considerably in the function
ascribed to the *avatar* by the puranic literature, the various popular cults,
the Krishnaite *bhakti*, etc. It is impossible to discuss any application of
this concept to the case of Christ without taking into account these variations in its meaning.

This is probably the place and the way in which light will gradually be thrown on the questions still left in suspense by what is incorrectly called the "Christian" theology of the "non-Christian" religions. Among these are that of the genuinely sacramental force which should be attributed to certain sacred signs outside the Judaeo-Christian system and that of the share of supernatural revelation, incomplete as it may be, which should be recognized in religious traditions outside this context. In this respect certain declarations show a notable increase in openmindedness. So the declaration of the International Theological Conference which met at Nagpur in India in the autumn of 1971 includes the following statement: "An ineffable mystery", definitively revealed and made known in Jesus Christ, "is in different forms and manners active among all peoples of the world and gives ultimate meaning to human existence and aspirations" (para. 13). "The self-communication of God is not confined to the Judaeo-Christian tradition, but extends to the whole of mankind in different ways and degrees within the one divine economy" (para. 14). "Since men who are saved attain their salvation in the context of their religious tradition the different sacred scriptures and rites of the religious traditions of the world can be in various degrees expressions of a divine manifestation and can be conducive to salvation. This in no way undermines the uniqueness of the Christian economy to which has been entrusted the decisive word spoken by Christ to the world and the means of salvation initiated by him" (para. 16).[4]

But such declarations, however open, will remain abstract and unconvincing as long as Christians are not prepared or are forbidden to expose themselves, in the freedom of the children of God, to the risk of spiritual encounters analogous to the one we have suggested. The person who lives in Christ and tries to let himself be led by the Spirit has fundamentally nothing to fear from these contemplative encounters once he has got over any initial upsets resulting from the breakdown of his accustomed frame of reference. It is to the glory of Christ, of a Christ even greater and more essential, that he will perhaps be amazed to

[4] *Evangelisation and Dialogue in India.* Report of the International Theological Conference held at Nagpur, India, 6–12 October 1971 (Nagpur, 1972), pp. 7–8.

hear the one Lord play his music on Krishna's flute. The theologians will come later and try to understand this expansion of frontiers. But they too are invited first to listen to the poem in silence.

Translated by Francis McDonagh

Biographical Notes

Joseph Beaude was born in 1933 and is a priest of the Oratory. *Licencié ès Lettres*, doctor of philosophy, he is doing research at the National Centre of Scientific Research (France). He has edited Robert Lenoble's *Histoire de l'idée de nature* (Paris, 1969) and has worked on a new edition of the *Œuvres* of Descartes. He is at present preparing a thesis for the *doctorat ès lettres* on *La crise culturelle au début du XVIIème siècle et le problème de Dieu*.

Albert-Marie Besnard, o.p., was born 27 March 1926 in Toulouse and ordained in 1954. Reader and licentiate in theology (at the Saulchoir), he has been editor of *La Vie Spirituelle* since 1969 and regular preacher at the broadcast Masses of France-Culture. Among his published works are: *Le pèlerinage chrétien* (Paris, 1959), *Saint Augustin: prier Dieu, les Psaumes* (Paris, 1964), *Visage spirituel des temps nouveaux* (Paris, 1964), *Le mystère du Nom* (*Quiconque invoquera le Nom du Seigneur sera sauvé* (Paris, 1962), *Vie et combats de la foi* (Paris, 1965), *Ces chrétiens que nous devenons* (Paris, 1967), *Un certain Jésus* (Paris, 1968), *Propos intempestifs sur la prière* (Paris, 1969) and *Chemins et Demeures* (Paris, 1972). He has regularly collaborated in the liturgical books *Assemblées du Seigneur*.

Bernard Besret was born 16 March 1935 in Brittany and entered the Cistercian monastery of Boquen in 1953. He studied philosophy and theology in Rome, gaining his doctorate of theology with a thesis on the subject *Incarnation ou eschatologie? Contribution à l'histoire du vocabulaire contemporain, 1935-1955* (Paris, 1964). Since 1970 he has been *animateur pastoral* of the group "Communion de Boquen". Among his published works, in addition to the thesis already mentioned, are: *Libération de l'homme. Essai sur le renouveau des valeurs monastiques* (Paris, 1969), *Clefs pour une nouvelle Eglise* (Paris, 1971), *Boquen hier, aujourd'hui et demain* (Paris, 1969), *Propos sur la liturgie* (Paris, 1970). He has also collaborated in the collective work *Les religieux aujourd'hui et demain* (Paris, 1964; Eng. trans. *Religious Orders in the Modern World*).

GÉRARD BESSIÈRE was born 27 January 1928 and ordained in 1951. He studied at the Institut Catholique, Paris, and at the Sorbonne (licentiate in theology and philosophy). After being at the service of priests and primary-school teachers in his diocese (Cahors) from 1953 to 1963 he became national chaplain of primary-school teachers. Among his published works are: *L'incognito de Dieu* (Paris, 1970) and *Des chrétiens de des mots* (Paris, 1971).

JOSEF BOMMER was born 26 March 1923 in Zürich and ordained in 1946. He studied at the Major Seminary of Coire and at the Angelicum, Rome. Doctor of theology, he is a parish priest in Zürich and assistant professor of pastoral theology at the Faculty of Theology, Lucerne. Among his published works are: *Beichtprobleme heute* (Zürich, 1968), *Plädoyer für die Freiheit* (Zürich, 1971), *Einübung ins Christlich* (Fribourg, 1970), *Vom Bèten des Christen* (Lucerne–Munich, 1963).

BRUNO BORCHERT, O.Carm., was born 4 February 1923 in Hengelo (Netherlands). He studied at the Dutch Carmelite Studium in Merkelbeek and at the Gregorian University, Rome. He is a doctor of theology. After teaching dogmatic theology at the Dutch Carmelite Theologicum and been responsible for the archives and iconographic collections there, he is now chief contributor to the review *Speling* and a contributor to the review *Kruispunt*. As well as various articles in many reviews, on iconography and spirituality, we owe to him the preparation of large dossiers on drugs, horizontalism, celibacy, Jesus of Nazareth, sexuality and mysticism.

LADISLAUS BOROS was born 2 October 1927 in Budapest. He entered the Society of Jesus and was ordained in 1957. He studied in Jesuit Houses in Hungary, Austria, Italy and France and also at the University of Munich, where he gained his doctorate in philosophy in 1954. He is assistant professor of the philosophy of religion at the University of Innsbruck. Among his published works are: *Mysterium Mortis—Der Mensch in der letzten Entscheidung* (Olten, 1971^9), *Der anwesende Gott* (Olten, 1972^8), *In der Versuchung. Meditationen über den Weg zur Vollendung* (Olten, 1972^5), *Aus der Hoffnung leben* (Olten, 1972^4), *Der gute Mensch und sein Gott* (Olten), 1971^2), *Erlöstes Dasein* (Mainz, 1968^{10}), *Im Menschen Gott begegnen* (Mainz, 1969^4), *Wir sind Zukunft* (Mainz, 1969) and *Der nahe Gott* (Mainz, 1971^2).

PIERRE-REGINALD CREN, O.P., was born 6 January 1932 in Lamballe (France) and ordained in 1958. He studied at the Dominican Studium of the Arbresle (Lyons), at the Faculties of the Saulchoir and at the Ecole Pratique de Hautes Etudes, Paris. Trained in Orientalism at the Indian Institute of Civilization, Paris, he assists at the Thomas-More Centre and is assistant professor at the Faculty of Theology of Lyons. He has written a number of articles, mainly in the review *Lumière et Vie*.

MICHEL DE GOEDT was born in 1924 in France and is a Discalced Carmelite, being ordained in 1949. He studied in Rome, Paris and Louvain. He has published articles of exegesis and *Foi au Christ et dialogues du chrétien* (Paris, 1967). He is carrying out research on theological questions concerning Judaism and the Jewish people.

PATRICK JACQUEMONT was born in 1932. After studying literature in Paris he entered the Dominican Order in 1954 and studied philosophy and theology at the Saulchoir, where he has been a professor since 1966. Specializing in patristic theology, he has also studied questions of the religious life, of prayer, of the sacrament of penance and of salvation. He has contributed to many reviews and collective works and his book *Oser prier* appeared in 1969. He is a collaborator with and theological adviser to many lay groups and movements in France.

JOSEPHINE MASSINGBERD FORD is associate professor of Sacred Scripture at the University of Notre Dame, Indiana, U.S.A. She gained bachelor's degrees in arts and theology, and a doctorate in philosophy in different English universities. Since 1967 she has been closely concerned with the Neo-Pentecostal Movement of Notre Dame.

JEAN-CLAUDE SAGNE, O.P., was born 16 May 1936 in Tours and was ordained in 1963. He made his theological studies at the Dominican Studium of the Arbresle. *Licencié ès lettres*, licentiate in theology and doctor of the third cycle in religious psychology he teaches psychology at the Catholic Faculties of Lyons and at the University of Lyons II. Among his published works is *Péché, culpabilité, pénitence* (Paris, 1971).